# DASH DIET ACTION PLAN

*Lower Your Blood Pressure and Lose Weight with the DASH Diet, 30-Day Meal Plan, and Over 75 Delicious Recipes!*

**Max Caligari**

Copyright © 2020 Max Caligari
All rights reserved. This book or parts thereof may not be reproduced in any form, stored in any retrieval system, or transmitted in any form by any means—electronic, mechanical, photocopy, recording, or otherwise—without prior written permission of the publisher.

# TABLE OF CONTENTS

Introduction ................................................................... 1

PART 1: EVERYTHING YOU NEED TO KNOW ........ 3

Chapter 1: About the Dash Diet ............................... 4
    What the DASH Diet Entails ............................. 10
Chapter 2: The First Month on the Dash Diet ............ 18
    Week One ......................................................... 25
    Week Two ......................................................... 27
    Week Three ....................................................... 29
    Week Four ........................................................ 31

PART 2: RECIPES ..................................................... 34

Chapter 3: Breakfast ................................................. 35
    Fluffy Whole-Wheat Biscuits ............................ 35
    Crock-Pot or Pressure Cooker Apple Pie Oatmeal 38
    Zucchini Bread ................................................. 40
    Oatmeal Applesauce Muffins ............................ 42
    Blueberry Oatmeal Bread ................................. 44
    Maple Banana Muffins ..................................... 46
    Waffles .............................................................. 48
    Breakfast Sausage Egg Casserole ..................... 50
    Bell Pepper Scrambled Eggs in a Hole ............ 52
    Blueberry Pancakes Mix ................................... 54
    Gluten-Free Pumpkin Pancakes ........................ 56
Chapter 4: Lunch and Dinner Entrees ....................... 58
    Taco Spaghetti Casserole ................................. 58
    Turkey Burgers ................................................. 61

- Zucchini Turkey Taco Boats ................................... 63
- Chicken Pineapple Kabobs ..................................... 66
- White Chicken Enchiladas ...................................... 68
- Pressure Cooker Red Beans and Rice ..................... 70
- Fettuccine Alfredo ................................................. 72
- Pesto Spaghetti Squash 'Pasta' ............................... 74
- Honey Lime Chicken .............................................. 76
- Roasted Carrot Soup .............................................. 78
- Garlic Broccoli Stir-Fry ......................................... 80
- Pan-Seared Cod in White Wine Tomato Basil Sauce ................................................................................ 82
- Creamy Mac and Cheese ....................................... 84
- Pulled Pork ............................................................ 86
- Turkey Chili .......................................................... 88
- Italian Chicken and Vegetables ............................. 90
- Tex Mex Chicken and Zucchini ............................ 92
- Turkey Meatloaf .................................................... 94
- Hamburger Goulash .............................................. 96
- Cabbage, Potato, and White Bean Soup ................ 98
- Sloppy Joes ......................................................... 100
- Creamy Tomato and Spinach Pasta ..................... 102

Chapter 5: Side Dishes ............................................. 104
- Wild Rice and Mushroom Pilaf ........................... 104
- Broccoli Gratin .................................................... 107
- California Vegetables with Parmesan Bread Crumbs ................................................................................ 109
- Rosemary and Parmesan Roasted Sweet Potatoes ................................................................................ 111
- Balsamic Spinach and Mushrooms ..................... 113
- Smashed Brussels Sprouts .................................. 115
- Mediterranean Chickpea Salad ........................... 117
- Thai Veggie 'Noodle' Salad ................................ 119
- Green Cabbage Cucumber Salad ........................ 121
- Lebanese Spicy Potatoes ..................................... 123
- Green Beans with Garlic and Onions .................. 125
- Honey Thyme Glazed Carrots ............................. 127

    Maple Roasted Beets and Carrots ....................... 129
Chapter 6: Snacks.............................................................. 131
    Baked Sweet Potato Chips ................................. 132
    Roasted Sugar Snap Peas .................................... 134
    Chili Lime Air Fryer Sweet Potatoes ................... 135
    Garlic Roasted Mushrooms .................................. 137
    Greek Lemon Potatoes ........................................ 139
    Broccoli and Cheddar Twice-Baked Potatoes ..... 141
    Broccoli Cauliflower Cheese Sticks..................... 144
    Quinoa Veggie Tots ............................................. 146
    Tomato Mozzarella Toast .................................... 148
    Parmesan Roasted Carrot Fries ........................... 150
    Frozen Banana Yoghurt Bites............................... 151
    Peanut Butter Energy Bites ................................. 152
    Cinnamon Apple Chips ....................................... 154
Chapter 7: Sauces, Gravies, and Seasonings................. 156
    Taco Seasoning.................................................... 156
    Marinara Sauce.................................................... 158
    Easy Homemade Salsa ........................................ 160
    Barbecue Sauce ................................................... 162
    Easy 5-Minute Gravy .......................................... 164
    Herbs de Provence Herb Seasoning .................... 165
    Teriyaki Sauce .................................................... 167
Chapter 8: Beverages ...................................................... 169
    Lavender Lemonade ............................................ 169
    Pink Drink Strawberry Refresher........................ 172
    Chocolate Banana Smoothie ............................... 173
    Coffee Banana Smoothie..................................... 175
    Cherry Limeade Detox Drink.............................. 177
Chapter 9: Desserts.......................................................... 178
    Oatmeal Chocolate Chip Cookies ....................... 179
    Fig Bars ............................................................... 182
    Whole-Grain Molasses Cookies.......................... 184
    Chocolate Peanut Butter Oatmeal No-Bake Cookies
    ............................................................................. 186
    Carrot Cake Banana Bread.................................. 188

Baked Pears with Walnuts............................................191
Conclusion ...................................................................193

# INTRODUCTION

What is the DASH diet? This diet stands for Dietary Approach to Stop Hypertension and has been around since the early 1990s. In fact, the DASH diet is so effective, that in 1992, the National Institute of Health (NIH) began to fund programs specifically using and targeting this diet plan.

As you may have guessed from the full name of the DASH diet, it is meant to specifically treat hypertension—in other words, high blood pressure. Studies have shown that you can reduce your blood pressure as much as many first-line blood pressure medicines, just by changing your eating habits. This is great news, especially as high blood pressure surges in many Western countries, increasing the risk of disease and mortality. Along with lowering your blood pressure and the associated risks, you can also improve your health in many other ways! Studies have found that the DASH diet can also reduce the risk of some of the most common disorders and diseases, such as diabetes, heart disease, cancer, stroke, osteoporosis, kidney stones, and heart failure. At the same time as you are improving your health, you can also lose weight, gain energy, and eat delicious and balanced meals.

By starting the DASH diet, studies have found that you can decrease your systolic blood pressure by eight to even fourteen points. This is a significant decrease, which you and your doctor can both be happy about! If your doctor is worried about your health, whether you have high blood pressure or are at risk of many of today's most common diseases, talk to them about beginning the DASH diet. One delicious meal at a time you can improve your health, lower your blood pressure, lose weight, and lead a more satisfying and fulfilling life.

Please remember, I am not a doctor and this book is not making medical claims or practicing medicine. You should always discuss anything related to medicine, health, or diet with your doctor before making any changes. This applies to all of the information in this book.

# PART 1
# EVERYTHING YOU
# NEED TO KNOW

# CHAPTER 1
# ABOUT THE DASH DIET

The DASH diet has been around for about thirty decades now, with it originating in the early 1990s. Because the diet showed so much promise for treating high blood pressure, early in its use in the year 1992, the National Institute of Health-funded studies and programs specifically to further utilize the diet. But, this isn't the end of the story, but only the beginning.

Later on, in 1996, the DASH diet was discussed in the American Heart Association's annual meeting. A year later, this led to the diet being published in the New England Journal of Medicine for its amazing benefits. After that, further studies were conducted on the DASH diet, resulting in the conclusion that the diet can have a great effect on lowering high blood pressure. And, these are only a handful of the early studies, as time has gone on more studies have been completed showing the amazing benefits the DASH diet offers. Not only have these studies found the diet to lower blood pressure, but also to reduce cellular DNA damage caused by oxidative stress, lower the risk of cardiovascular diseases, improve bone health, reduce the risk of heart failure, reduce insulin resistance and type II diabetes, and more. A study of the diet completed in 2017 found that if individuals with high blood pressure faithfully follow the DASH diet plan, then it could potentially prevent 400,000 deaths caused by cardiovascular disease over a ten year period.

In short, the DASH diet has been proven to offer powerful, long-lasting, and full-body effects against many of today's most troubling ailments. Whether you have high blood pressure or not, you can likely benefit by implementing this diet in your daily life. You can choose to use this diet to treat high blood pressure, improve overall health and potential life expectancy, or just to lose weight. That is what is great about this plan—it is easy to maintain, full of delicious and balanced meals, can be practiced by a large portion of the population, and it has many benefits.

You may be reading this book because your doctor has told you that you have high blood pressure and need to lower it. However, some people suspect they may have high blood pressure, but have not talked about it with their doctor yet. For others, it may simply be a confusing subject, as many people don't explain it in simple everyday terms for the layperson. Let me first say that you should always discuss this with your doctor. If you haven't yet, make an appointment to do so.

When your doctor discusses blood pressure, they may not go into specific or they may use overly complicated terms. Don't worry, I am here to help! Blood pressure doesn't have to be a confusing subject, you can understand it so that you can come to better understand your own health and well-being. After all, while it is important that we listen to and consult our doctors, we are also our own best advocate, so listen to your body and its needs while also heeding the wise counsel of your physician. If you don't trust your doctor, that is okay, you can always try getting a second opinion from another doctor. Thankfully, the subject of blood pressure is pretty straightforward in medical terms, so your doctor will likely have a good handle on the situation. But, if you are uncomfortable seeing a general practitioner regarding your blood pressure and heart health, you may try seeing a cardiologist instead, as they specialize in treating the heart.

Now, one of the most common confusions regarding blood pressure is what the numbers mean. There are two sets of numbers, a top and a bottom one. But, you may be wondering what the difference is and how they impact your health. The top or first number is known as systolic blood pressure. With this number, doctors are able to determine how much pressure is being pushed against the arteries from your blood every time your heartbeats.

The bottom or second number is diastolic blood pressure. While the systolic number measures how much pressure is on your arteries every time the heartbeats, the diagnostic measures how much pressure there is when the heart is at rest between beats.

Because the systolic number measures how much pressure is against your arteries when your heart is at work, this number is going to be higher and more indicative of risk and disease. While your doctor will keep an eye on both your systolic and diastolic blood pressure, it will be the systolic blood pressure that they are most concerned about, especially in middle age and elderly people. This is because as a person ages their arteries build up plaque and become stiff, which increases the pressure of the blood flow, thereby increasing the risk of heart attack and disease.

However, while a doctor may focus on the systolic pressure in general, there are exceptions. Either a high systolic or diastolic number can indicate high blood pressure, studies have shown that with every 20mm increase in systolic pressure or 10mm in diastolic blood pressure people experience increased risk of disease. In fact, for every 20mm or 10mm rise in pressure, a person's risk of death from a heart-related event or stroke doubles for people over the age of forty.

The American Heart Association recognizes five blood pressure ranges, each with their own level of risk in relation to heart health. Let's take a look at each, in turn, as if you want to lower your blood pressure with the DASH diet it is imperative to understand how your blood pressure works, where it is at, and your goal blood pressure range.

- Normal

While any reduction in blood pressure is good if you have high blood pressure, your end-goal should be to get into the normal or safe range. In general, anything under 120mm systolic and 80mm diastolic is considered normal. Having your blood pressure in this range is ideal for your heart health. Although you don't want your blood pressure to go under 90mm systolic and 60mm diastolic, as that is classified as low blood pressure, which causes its own set of problems.

- Elevated

Blood pressure is considered elevated when the systolic number is within 120-129mm while the diastolic is no higher than 80mm. While elevated blood pressure is not yet classified as high blood pressure, people with chronically elevated blood pressure are likely to develop high blood pressure. It is recommended to begin lowering it back to normal now, to prevent high blood pressure and its associated risks.

- High Blood Pressure, Stage 1

Also known as hypertension, this is the first stage of high blood pressure. During this stage, the systolic number will range between 130mm and 139mm, while the diastolic number will range between 80mm and 89mm. During this stage of high blood pressure, your doctor is likely to recommend lifestyle changes, such as the DASH diet, exercise, and other healthy habits. They may even consider adding in blood pressure medication now or in the near future if your situation doesn't improve, in order to reduce the risk of heart attack and stroke.

- High Blood Pressure Stage 2

When a person is in the second stage of hypertension, their blood pressure will regularly maintain a 140mm systolic and 90mm diastolic number, or higher. This stage of high blood pressure is dangerous, and the danger increases the more the number increases. At this stage, a doctor is more likely to immediately put their patients on medication and recommend more drastic lifestyle changes. High blood pressure should never be taken lightly, but this is especially true of stage two.

- Hypertensive Crisis

When blood pressure gets critically high, it is known as hypertensive crisis. This is an incredibly dangerous state. Sometimes, it can occur due to acute medical trauma or medical treatment. For instance, someone who has gone into an allergic reaction known as anaphylaxis and been injected with epinephrine to stop the reaction will experience acute high blood pressure. Their blood pressure may spike into a hypertensive crisis, until the allergic reaction in under control, and the effects of the epinephrine have worn off.

However, some people may have chronic high blood pressure that gets so bad that it reaches a hypertensive crisis. If you reach a hypertensive crisis wait five minutes and test your blood pressure again. If your blood pressure is still in this range, then call your doctor immediately and seek medical care. This is vital, as a hypertensive crisis can cause organ damage, shortness of breath, back and chest pains, weakness, difficulty speaking or seeing, and more.

What numbers qualify as a hypertensive crisis? That would be when the systolic number reaches 180mm or higher and the diastolic number is 120mm or higher.

While the main goal of the DASH diet may be to reduce blood pressure, that is not the only goal. Remember, this diet plan has many health benefits, which is why it is regularly recommended by doctors. One of the great health benefits is that it can help people lose weight.

While this diet is not usually used only for weight loss, you can lose weight as it is a balanced and healthy lifestyle plan. But, at the same time, if you are already at a healthy weight or underweight, you can easily maintain weight as well. This is because you will still largely eat the same foods.

If you want to try losing weight with the DASH diet, try these tips:

- Reduce portion size and daily calorie consumption.
- Prioritize vegetables and fruit consumption rather than meat and grains.
- Rather than calorie-dense snack foods and desserts, choose vegetables and fruits as snacks.

## What the DASH Diet Entails

Now that we have looked into the importance of the DASH diet and what it can do, it is time to dig deeper into what exactly the diet entails and how you can follow the plan. If you ever find yourself confused about what the diet does and doesn't 'allow,' then refer back to this section to review the details again.

First, it is important to understand there are two versions of the DASH diet. There is the Standard DASH diet and the Low-Sodium DASH diet. For convenience sake, when I mention the DASH diet I am specifically referring to the Standard version. On the other hand, when speaking of the Low-Sodium version, I will specify which version I am speaking of.

On the Standard Dash diet, a person reduces their sodium intake and consumes no more than 2,300mg (milligrams) of sodium daily. This sodium intake is already considered 'low,' but the Low-Sodium DASH diet reduces it further. In this version, a person consumes no more than 1,500mg daily.

Both versions of the DASH diet have their benefits. Which version a person chooses should depend on how severe their health is and whichever version their doctor recommends. Your doctor may recommend the Low-Sodium version if your blood pressure is especially high or you are at a greater risk of complications.

Along with reducing sodium intake, the DASH diet also increases a person's potassium intake. This is helpful, as potassium can help lower blood pressure by relaxing the blood vessels. In general, a person should aim to consume about

4,700mg daily. However, again, you should always discuss your diet with your doctor and make sure it is safe to consume this potassium level with your specific health.

Some high-potassium foods include:

- Potatoes
- Sweet Potatoes
- Pumpkin
- Cucumbers
- Zucchini
- Eggplant
- Mushrooms
- Peas
- Leafy Greens
- Cooked Broccoli
- Cooked Spinach
- Kidney Beans
- Lentils
- Orange Juice
- Bananas
- Dried Apricots
- Prunes
- Raisins

Along with prioritizing reduced sodium and increased potassium intake, the DASH diet also promotes a focus on fruits, vegetables, and low-fat dairy. You can also consume whole grains, poultry, fish, nuts, and seeds, but these should be consumed in moderation.

You may occasionally enjoy some fats, sweets, and red meat, but only in small amounts. Overall, the DASH diet is a low-fat diet, so when you do eat fats you should prioritize healthy fats such as those from nuts, seeds, and vegetables. These types of fats are heart-healthy, whereas animal-based fats are known to raise blood pressure and artery plaque buildup.

Let's look at how the DASH diet could look in your daily life with each of the main food groups you will be eating. A person's specific calorie recommendation will vary based on many factors. You can ask your doctor about this, as well, as they will be able to determine your caloric intake needs better than online calculators. But, for the sake of convenience, we will be looking at these food groups using a 2,000 caloric intake model, as it is a pretty standard intake.

Whole Grains

When consuming grains, you should always try to find whole grains. This is because refined grains cause a spike in blood sugar, insulin, and have less nutrition. This means if you can choose, pick brown rice over white, whole wheat flour over bleached, whole-wheat pasta over regular, and whole-grain breakfast cereal rather than heavily refined varieties. Usually, whole grain products will specifically mention being whole-grain or whole-wheat, so look for these labels.

While whole grains are full of nutrients and have moderate calorie content, they are also great because they are naturally low in fat! But, you need to be careful to keep them this way, as many people add in butter, oil, cream cheese, and other high-fat additions.

In general, you should aim to consume six to eight servings of whole grains a day. This includes a half cup of pasta or cooked cereals such as rice or buckwheat, a slice of bread, one ounce of dried cereals. Keep in mind, when discussing cereals these are not the same as breakfast cereals you can purchase at the grocery store to eat with milk. Instead, cereals generally refined to grains that you can cook in water, such as rice, buckwheat, millet, or quinoa.

Vegetables

Many people simply think of vegetables as a side dish, but you should prioritize them as the main part of your diet. You can roast or steam them and then pair them with whole grains for a delicious and balanced meal. It is advised to specifically choose the high-potassium vegetables, such as the ones listed earlier in this chapter, but you can still eat other vegetables, as well.

When purchasing vegetables, it is best to choose fresh and frozen varieties, as these won't have any added sodium unless they are prepared with a sauce or seasoning. Avoid the types that have been prepared in such a way, and instead, choose vegetables without any added ingredients. If you choose to purchase canned vegetables, only purchase those that are low-sodium or without any added so salt, as canned foods are notoriously high in sodium.

In general, you want to consume between four to six servings of vegetables daily. A single serving would include a cup of raw vegetables or half a cup of cooked vegetables.

Fruits

Fruits are a great way to add more flavor and sweetness to your daily life. If you are craving a sweet treat, instead of reaching for a dessert, try a serving of fruit! You can be surprised how well some plums, cherries, or mango can hit the sweet spot. Of course, you should still eat fruit in moderation because it contains natural sugars, but it also contains plenty of fiber and vitamins.

When possible, you will want to eat the peel of fruits such as apples, pears, and grapes, as many of the nutrients are found in the peels. Ask your doctor if citrus juice is safe for you, especially grapefruit, as it can interfere with certain medications. Of course, when choosing canned fruit or juice, choose options without any added sugar.

You should aim for four to five servings of fruit a day. A serving can vary depending on the source, such as half a cup of chopped up fruit, one medium-sized piece of fruit, or four ounces of juice.

Dairy

A great addition to your daily is dairy, as it is a major source of protein, calcium, and vitamin D. However, this does not mean you can eat endless dairy or purchase any variety. You should stick with low-fat or fat-free varieties, as dairy is a large source of saturated fat, which will worsen your heart health in large quantities. You also want to avoid varieties will high levels of sodium, so keep cheese limited. If you are lactose-intolerant, then you might choose varieties that are lactose-free, or purchase lactase enzyme tablets.

Two to three daily servings of dairy a day are allowed, with a serving consisting of one cup of low-fat yogurt or skim milk or one and a half ounces of low-fat cheese.

### Lean Meat and Fish

Protein is an important part of a balanced diet and is also a great source of vitamins and minerals. On the DASH diet, you want to choose lean meats, with poultry and fish being your go-to options. While you generally want to eat low-fat meats, fish such as salmon contain heart-healthy fats and omega-3 that are good for you. Try to eat fatty fish at least once a week.

You can also enjoy eggs, but remember that eggs contain saturated fat, so if you want to eat them in larger quantities you may want to remove some of or all of the yolks.

When eating proteins, you can have six servings a day. A serving of meat is one ounce of cooked meat or fish or one egg.

### Legumes, Nuts, and Seeds

This section of the DASH diet food pyramid contains many powerful plant-based nutrients, including protein. Many of these foods, such as walnuts, hemp seeds, and soybeans, contain nutrients that have been proven through many studies to have numeral health benefits. In fact, in many of these studies, people who regularly consume a moderate amount of the foods in this category are able to lose more weight and experience improved health—including heart health.

Consume foods in this category four to five times a week, as they are higher in calories. One serving would consist of half a cup of cooked beans or peas, one third a cup of chopped nuts, or two tablespoons of nut or seed butter.

### Fat and Oil

While you may want to restrict your fat consumption to improve your heart health, fat is still an important part of your diet in moderation. It is through fat that your body is able to strengthen the immune system and absorb vital vitamins. While you will limit your fat on this diet, the biggest factor is what types of fat you are eating. For instance, if two people on the DASH diet both ate the same amount of fat, but one at unsaturated fats while the other ate saturated, then the person who experienced the benefits would obviously be the one who chose the heart-healthy unsaturated fats.

On the DASH diet, no more than thirty percent of your calories should originate from fat. This means if you have two-thousand calories a day, then no more than six-hundred should be from fat. While this may sound like a lot, and it is, it is important to keep track of because fat is higher in calories than other foods, meaning you can reach this threshold much more quickly than you might think.

Do your best to limit saturated fats, as found in meat, eggs, dairy, coconut oil, palm oil, shortening, and lard. Avoid trans fats completely, which are found in fried and processed foods. Instead, choose unsaturated fats, prioritizing monounsaturated fats. Some great options include extra virgin olive oil, avocado, nuts, seeds, olives, soy products, and fatty fish.

In general, you should choose two to three servings of fat a day. A serving might be a teaspoon of oil, butter, or margarine; a tablespoon of mayonnaise; or two tablespoons of salad dressing.

Sweets

You should limit yourself to only small portions of sweets a week. But, what qualifies as a 'small' portion? This can be confusing, as for some people this may be almost no sugar whatsoever while another drinks a lot of soda. In this case, you can allow yourself to have a glass of lemonade, a scoop of sorbet, or even a tablespoon of sugar or jam.

You can have these types of sweets five times or fewer a week. When you do eat them, try to make them of the healthier variety, or at least low-fat. You can also use sugar replacements in moderation.

Caffeine and Alcohol

Caffeine isn't addressed on the DASH diet, largely because the long-term effects of caffeine on blood pressure are unknown. However, it is proven that caffeine can temporarily affect blood pressure, so you should be careful. Discuss your caffeine consumption with your doctor and stick with their recommendation.

In excess, alcohol can raise blood pressure. The American guidelines recommend no more than two drinks a day for men and no more than one for women. However, again, you should discuss this with your doctor, as alcohol negatively interacts with many health conditions and medications.

# CHAPTER 2

# THE FIRST MONTH ON

# THE DASH DIET

Even if blood pressure is only slightly elevated, it can become unhealthy if it remains in this elevated zone long-term. This damage is only worsened the higher your blood pressure is, greatly increasing your risk of heart attack, stroke, and other life-threatening medical conditions. Thankfully, you don't have to throw your hands up and accept this as 'inevitable.' Instead, you can make a change for the better, improving your heart health and your entire life. With the DASH diet, long-tested and commonly recommended by doctors and scientists, you can lower your blood pressure, improve your heart health, and improve your life.

In the previous chapter, we analyzed how many servings you should eat in a week or a day of the most common food groups. You can refer back to that chapter whenever you need a reminder of how to structure your day-to-day eating habits. But, now let's look at a more precise measurement with specific set numbers so that you can see a more concrete version of what the DASH diet should look like. This example follows the same dietary intake of individuals partaking in DASH diet study programs, which means you can trust that it is effective. While everyone will have their own caloric intake recommendation, which your doctor can provide you, this eating plan example is based on a person with a 2,100 caloric intake. If your caloric intake is different, yours will look slightly different, but the percentages should still remain the same.

- Total Fat: 27% calories
- Saturated Fat: 6% calories
- Protein: 18% calories
- Carbohydrates: 55% calories
- Cholesterol: 150mg
- Sodium: 2,300mg
- Potassium: 4,700 mg
- Calcium: 1,250 mg
- Magnesium: 500 mg
- Fiber: 30 g

As mentioned in the first chapter, there are two versions of the DASH Diet, the standard and the low-sodium. While many people use the standard DASH diet, the low-sodium version has been found to be particularly helpful for those with excessively high blood pressure, the elderly, those with underlying health conditions, and African Americans. Again, for the standard version, 2,300mg of sodium is recommended, whereas, for the low-sodium version, 1,500mg is recommended.

You can use the DASH diet to either lose weight or maintain

weight, making it incredibly versatile. This is important, because some people with high blood pressure are already at their recommended weight, and shouldn't lose any more. On the other hand, many others with high blood pressure are recommended to lose weight to improve their heart health. So, what should you do if you need to lose weight on the DASH diet? All you have to do is reduce your caloric intake, which is incredibly easy. Your doctor can recommend a caloric intake that will help you to lose weight while still eating enough, so be sure to discuss the matter with them.

There are many ways you can reduce your caloric intake, here are a few tips:

- Reduce your overall fat intake, as fat is high in calories.
- Enjoy fresh fruit rather than desserts.
- Eat vegetable-based snacks rather than high caloric alternatives.
- Replace a portion of your meal's meat and grains with low-carb vegetables.
- Take it easy on added condiments, snacking, and other frequently overlooked calories.
- Slowly reduce your meal portion size.
- Remember to read food labels.
- Avoid sugar
- Reduce processed food intake, even low-fat and low-sodium foods.
- Drink more water

Along with reducing your caloric intake if you are trying to lose weight, everyone on the DASH diet will need to learn to reduce their sodium intake. This will be simple by following the recipes in this book, but there are a few simple methods you need to keep in mind. These are:

- Rely mostly on fresh and frozen produce.
- If using canned foods, be sure that they are low-sodium or no-salt-added versions. Standard canned foods are notoriously high in sodium.
- Use fresh lean meats and fish, rather than canned, smoked, and processed varieties.
- Reduce cured, brined, and smoked foods such as ham, bacon, pickles, and olives.
- Limit condiments, and choose low-sodium varieties.
- Limit even low-sodium versions of soy sauce and teriyaki sauce.
- Rinse canned foods before eating them.
- Purchase low-sodium broth, or make your own homemade broth to reduce the sodium content even further.
- Use a variety of herbs and spices rather than salt.

It is important to learn how to read nutritional labels, as you should always examine them when purchasing food. These labels will give you insight into how much sodium is in food, as well as the fat sources, calories, potassium, and anything else you might need to keep in mind.

When looking for the sodium content on the nutritional label you want to choose products that have five percent or less of your daily value of sodium. Alternatively, a product is considered high-sodium if it contains twenty percent or more of your daily value. For instance, if you look at canned tomatoes, you will find that a regular can of diced tomatoes tend to contain approximately nine percent of your daily sodium value. However, a can of no-salt-added tomatoes only contains one percent of your daily value. This goes to show how important it is to not only choose your ingredients wisely but also to regularly read the nutritional labels.

Look at these two varieties of canned tomato nutritional labels. Both are by the same brand, with the only difference being one is regular and one is no salt added.

When reading product labels, there are certain commonly used phrases. However, these phrases are not used randomly, they have specific meanings. The meanings of these phrases are overseen by the government so that everyone abides by them. This is helpful to know because you can then understand the difference of sodium-free compared to low-sodium.

Let's look at some commonly used phrases and their meanings:

- Sodium-free or salt-free = Less than 5mg sodium
- Very low sodium = 35mg or less of sodium
- Low-sodium = 140mg or less of sodium
- Reduced sodium or less sodium = 25% or less sodium than the regular version
- Light sodium = 50% or less sodium than the regular version
- No salt added = While the food is not sodium-free, no salt was added during production

- Fat-free = 0.5g or less fat
- Low saturated fat = 1g or less and 15% or less of the calories originate from saturated fat
- Low-fat = 3g or less of fat
- Reduced-fat = 25% or less fat than the regular version
- Light in fat = 50% or less fat than the regular version.

Along with making gradual changes to adopt the DASH diet, watching what you eat, and reading nutritional labels, it is also recommended to incorporate exercise into your daily life. Countless studies have found that just thirty minutes of moderate exercise can greatly help in reducing blood pressure. This means that you can simply go on a short walk, workout at the gym, or even just use a jump rope outdoors. The options are really limitless, just find a simple aerobic exercise that fits your needs. Not only will this help you lose weight and reduce blood pressure, but if you take any blood pressure medication it will also help it work more effectively, as shown in studies.

As you can see, the DASH diet is not difficult, you can easily implement these simple changes into your lifestyle and diet. You don't even have to make all the changes at once. You can make small changes one day at a time until you reach a set goal. For instance, you might start out with just lowering your sodium intake and then slowly work on also reducing your fat intake, improving your caloric intake, implementing exercise, and so on. Find a way to implement it that works for you, it doesn't have to be difficult.

Now that you understand how to implement the DASH diet, let's look at a simple 30-day meal plan that you can use to get started! While reading this menu plan, please keep in mind that you can alter this plan to fit your needs. The sodium and calorie count calculated for this plan are with the base serving size implemented. However, you can increase the serving size, add in more snacks, or add side dishes to increase the caloric intake to fit your needs.

# Week One

| | Breakfast | Lunch | Dinner | Snack/Dessert | Sodium Total | Calorie Total |
|---|---|---|---|---|---|---|
| Sunday | Waffles | Pressure Cooker Red Beans and Rice | Turkey Meatloaf | Oatmeal Chocolate Chip Cookies | 133mg | 797 |
| Monday | Blueberry Oatmeal Bread | Creamy Mac and Cheese | Honey Lime Chicken | Tomato Mozzarella Toast | 682mg | 1,077 |
| Tuesday | Bell Pepper Scrambled Eggs in a Hole | Turkey Burgers | Fettuccine Alfredo | Roasted Sugar Snap Peas | 209mg | 633 |
| Wednesday | Fluffy Whole-Wheat Biscuits | Garlic Broccoli Stir-Fry | Sloppy Joes | Garlic Roasted Mushrooms | 649mg | 771 |

| Thursday | Breakfast Sausage Egg Casserole | Turkey Chili | Pan-Seared Cod in White Wine Tomato Basil Sauce | Baked Sweet Potato Chips | 1019 mg | 774 |
| --- | --- | --- | --- | --- | --- | --- |
| Friday | Waffles | Roasted Carrot Soup | Creamy Tomato and Spinach Pasta | Greek Lemon Potatoes | 321mg | 978 |
| Saturday | Crock-Pot or Pressure Cooker Apple Pie Oatmeal | Tex Mex Chicken and Zucchini | Hamburger Goulash | Broccoli and Cheddar Twice-Baked Potatoes | 543mg | 1080 |

# Week Two

| | Breakfast | Lunch | Dinner | Snack/Dessert | Sodium Total | Calorie Total |
|---|---|---|---|---|---|---|
| Sunday | Blueberry Pancakes Mix | Turkey Chili | Pan-Seared Cod in White Wine Tomato Basil Sauce | Fig Bars | 699 mg | 1002 |
| Monday | Bell Pepper Scrambled Eggs in a Hole | Creamy Mac and Cheese | Cabbage, Potato, and White Bean Soup | Baked Sweet Potato Chips | 395 mg | 1015 |
| Tuesday | Oatmeal Applesauce Muffins | Sloppy Joes | Chicken Pineapple Kabobs | Broccoli Cauliflower Cheese Sticks | 651 mg | 788 |
| Wednesday | Bell Pepper Scrambled Eggs in a Hole | Fettuccine Alfredo | Italian Chicken and Vegetables | Quinoa Veggie Tots | 359 mg | 957 |

| | | | | | | |
|---|---|---|---|---|---|---|
| Thursday | Blueberry Pancakes Mix | Turkey Burgers | Taco Spaghetti Casserole | Parmesan Roasted Carrot Fries | 546 mg | 744 |
| Friday | Maple Banana Muffins | Zucchini Turkey Taco Boats | Creamy Tomato and Spinach Pasta | Frozen Banana Yoghurt Bites | 607 mg | 937 |
| Saturday | Zucchini Bread | Hamburger Goulash | Pulled Pork | Cinnamon Apple Chips | 171 mg | 979 |

# DASH DIET ACTION PLAN

## Week Three

| | Breakfast | Lunch | Dinner | Snack/Dessert | Sodium Total | Calorie Total |
|---|---|---|---|---|---|---|
| Sunday | Gluten-Free Pumpkin Pancakes | Turkey Burgers | Creamy Tomato and Spinach Pasta | Chocolate Peanut Butter Oatmeal No-Bake Cookies | 262 | 887 |
| Monday | Zucchini Bread | Roasted Carrot Soup | Sloppy Joes | Garlic Roasted Mushrooms | 292 mg | 765 |
| Tuesday | Fluffy Whole-Wheat Biscuits | Turkey Chili | Honey Lime Chicken | Greek Lemon Potatoes | 467 mg | 671 |
| Wednesday | Crock-Pot or Pressure Cooker Apple Pie Oatmeal | Pressure Cooker Red Beans and Rice | Fettuccine Alfredo | Baked Sweet Potato Chips | 2164 mg | 835 |

| Thursday | Oatmeal Applesauce Muffins | Garlic Broccoli Stir-Fry | Hamburger Goulash | Broccoli and Cheddar Twice-Baked Potatoes | 833 mg | 1194 |
| Friday | Bell Pepper Scrambled Eggs in a Hole | Creamy Mac and Cheese | Turkey Meatloaf | Roasted Sugar Snap Peas | 129 mg | 787 |
| Saturday | Waffles | Tex Mex Chicken and Zucchini | Cabbage, Potato, and White Bean Soup | Tomato Mozzarella Toast | 827 mg | 1150 |

# Week Four

| | Breakfast | Lunch | Dinner | Snack/Dessert | Sodium Total | Calorie Total |
|---|---|---|---|---|---|---|
| Sunday | Breakfast Sausage Egg Casserole | Pesto Spaghetti Squash 'Pasta' | Cabbage, Potato, and White Bean Soup | Carrot Cake Banana Bread | 736 mg | 961 |
| Monday | Maple Banana Muffins | Garlic Broccoli Stir-Fry | Taco Spaghetti Casserole | Quinoa Veggie Tots | 909 mg | 1220 |
| Tuesday | Blueberry Oatmeal Bread | Creamy Mac and Cheese | Pulled Pork | Broccoli Cauliflower Cheese Sticks | 289 mg | 1118 |
| Wednesday | Zucchini Bread | Sloppy Joes | White Chicken Enchiladas | Garlic Roasted Mushrooms | 595 mg | 924 |

| | | | | | | |
|---|---|---|---|---|---|---|
| Thursday | Oatmeal Applesauce Muffins | Zucchini Turkey Taco Boats | Creamy Tomato and Spinach Pasta | Parmesan Roasted Carrot Fries | 645 mg | 926 |
| Friday | Bell Pepper Scrambled Eggs in a Hole | Turkey Burgers | Roasted Carrot Soup | Cinnamon Apple Chips | 228 mg | 445 |
| Saturday | Crock-Pot or Pressure Cooker Apple Pie Oatmeal | Hamburger Goulash | Italian Chicken and Vegetables | Frozen Banana Yoghurt Bites | 356 mg | 805 |
| Sunday | Waffles | Turkey Chili | Chicken Pineapple Kabobs | Baked Pears with Walnuts | 462 mg | 895 |
| Monday | Fluffy Whole-Wheat Biscuits | Fettuccine Alfredo | Pan-Seared Cod in White Wine Tomato Basil Sauce | Baked Sweet Potato Chips | 497 mg | 1049 |

# PART 2
# RECIPES

# CHAPTER 3

# BREAKFAST

Breakfast has long been considered the most important meal of the day. Why is this? Breakfast isn't a magical meal where the calories and nutrients affect your body differently than other times of the day. However, studies have found breakfast to be the most important in whether you are setting yourself up for success or failure. If you start out with a poor breakfast, you are more likely to continue eating poorly throughout the day. On the other hand, if you start out with a healthy and filling balanced breakfast, you are more likely to continue making healthy choices and experience greater success on your diet. The recipes in this chapter are just what you need to get your day started on the right track.

## Fluffy Whole-Wheat Biscuits

Enjoy these biscuits sweet or savory, with your favorite jams and jellies, eggs and turkey, or even your favorite southern gravy. However you serve these biscuits, you are sure to love them! Rather than using regular whole-wheat flour, these biscuits specifically use whole-wheat pastry flour for in incredibly light and fluffy texture.

**The Servings:** 10

**The Time to Prepare/Cook:** 20 minutes

**The Calories:** 134

**The Sodium:** 49mg

**The Potassium:** 327mg

**The Ingredients:**

Whole-wheat pastry flour – 2 cups

Low-sodium baking powder – 4 teaspoons

Butter, cold – .25 cup

Low-fat buttermilk, cold – 1 cup

**The Instructions:**

1. Allow your often to warm to Fahrenheit 450 degrees while you prepare the biscuits. Also line a baking sheet with a silicone mat or kitchen parchment.

2. In a medium bowl, combine together the low-sodium baking powder with the whole-wheat flour. Don't skip this step, otherwise you will end up with nasty baking powder clumps in your biscuits.

3. Slice the cold butter into the flour and use a pastry cutter to work the two together. The butter should eventually form pea-sized clumps coated in the flour. This step allows your biscuits to become tender and flaky. Ensure the butter is cold, otherwise it won't hold up. Stir in the buttermilk, just until combined. Don't over work the dough once the buttermilk is added.

4. Transfer the dough onto a clean flour-covered surface. Sprinkle a little flour over the top of the dough and roll it out with a rolling pin until it is about one inch in thickness. Use a round cookie-cutter or medium-sized glass rim to cut the biscuits into evenly-sized rounds. Transfer the rounds to the prepared baking sheet so that each biscuit is about an inch apart.

5. With any extra dough, pres it back together, roll it out again, and cut out the remaining biscuits. Continue doing this until you have used up all the dough. Avoid overcrowding your baking pan, you can cook the biscuits in two batches or use two pans to do this.

6. Bake the biscuits in the center of the heated oven until fluffy and golden-brown in color, about ten to twelve minutes. Remove from the oven and serve while warm or store for later.

## Crock-Pot or Pressure Cooker Apple Pie Oatmeal

This oatmeal is great, as you can easily prepare it in the evening and wake up in the morning with a warm, delicious, and comforting breakfast for the entire family. These only take a few minutes to prepare, saving you time.

Of course, if you are unable to prepare these the night before, you can also cook them in only a few minutes the morning of if you have an electric pressure cooker.

**The Servings:** 8

**The Time to Prepare/Cook:** 17 minutes

**The Calories:** 196

**The Sodium:** 5mg

**The Potassium:** 213mg

**The Ingredients:**

Steel-cut oats – 2 cups

Water – 7 cups

Vanilla extract - .75 teaspoon

Apples, diced – 2

Nutmeg, ground - .25 teaspoon

Ginger, ground - .25 teaspoon

Cinnamon, ground - .5 teaspoon

**The Instructions:**

1. Stir together all of the ingredients in the lining of a

crock-pot or electric pressure cooker.

2. If you are using a crock-pot, allow it to cook on low for six to eight hours overnight. If you are using an electric pressure cooker, set the cooking time to manual for ten to thirteen minutes. The longer you cook the oats, the creamier they will be.

3. Serve the oats warm, plain, or with a little pure maple syrup, brown sugar, or a sweetener alternative.

## Zucchini Bread

This bread is warm, comforting, and delicious. If you have never had zucchini bread, you will be surprised by the amazing texture and sweet flavor it gives the bread. Due to the high moisture content of this bread, it can only be stored at room temperature for two or three days. Although, you can store it in the fridge for up to a week.

**The Servings:** 10

**The Time to Prepare/Cook:** 70 minutes

**The Calories:** 268

**The Sodium:** 21mg

**The Potassium:** 252mg

**The Ingredients:**

While whole-wheat flour – 1.75 cup

Nutmeg, ground - .25 teaspoon

Low-sodium baking powder – 1 teaspoon

Cinnamon, ground – 1 teaspoon

Vanilla extract – 2 teaspoons

Honey - .5 cup

Skim milk - .5 cup

Extra virgin olive oil - .33 cup

Walnuts, chopped - .75 cup

Eggs – 2

Zucchini, grated – 1.5 cups

**The Instructions:**

1. Start by setting the oven to Fahrenheit 325 degrees, setting the oven's rack to the center shelf, and lining a nine-by-five inch loaf pan with kitchen parchment. If you don't have kitchen parchment, then you can grease the pan with oil and sprinkle some flour inside to coat it to prevent sticking.

2. Whisk together the honey with the olive oil, before adding in the eggs. Ensure the ingredients are well combined before stirring in the vanilla, nutmeg, cinnamon, low-sodium baking powder, and skim milk.

3. Stir the flour into the wet mixture just until combined. There may be some clumps, but that is okay. Now, gently fold in the grated zucchini and the chopped walnuts. Pour the batter into the prepared baking pan.

4. Bake the zucchini bread until it is cooked through all the way and a toothpick or knife once inserted into the center of the loaf is removed clean—about an hour. Remove the zucchini bread from the oven and allow it to cool in the loaf pan for ten minutes. Now, run a spatula or knife along the edges to release it from the metal and invert it so that the loaf is removed from the pan. Allow it to cool on a wire rack for at least twenty minutes, or until room-temperature, before slicing.

# Oatmeal Applesauce Muffins

These muffins are a great addition to your morning routine. They are great to prepare ahead of time, as you can store them in the pantry, fridge, or even freezer until you plan to enjoy them. While they may not be as quick as some other breakfast option, keep in mind that most of the preparation and cooking time doesn't require hands-on work.

**The Servings:** 6

**The Time to Prepare/Cook:** 60 minutes

**The Calories:** 283

**The Sodium:** 61mg

**The Potassium:** 435mg

**The Ingredients:**

Whole wheat flour – 1 cup

Low-sodium baking powder – 1.5 teaspoons

Rolled oats – 1 cup

Cinnamon, ground – 1 teaspoon

Low-fat buttermilk, room temperature – 1 cup

Egg, room temperature – 1

Applesauce, unsweetened – .5 cup

Dark brown sugar - .5 cup

**The Instructions:**

1. Begin by setting your oven to Fahrenheit 375 degrees and lining a regular size muffin tray with paper liners. You should have twelve lined muffin cups in total.

2. In a small bowl, combine together the oats and the buttermilk, stirring until the oats are fully coated. Allow the two to sit for twenty minutes so that the oats soften.

3. In a large bowl, combine together the cinnamon, low-sodium baking powder, flour, and brown sugar. Once combined, stir in the apple sauce, egg, and the buttermilk-oat mixture. Stir until there are no lumps remaining, but being careful to not over mix.

4. Divide the batter between the twelve muffin cups, being careful to not fill any of the cups more than three-quarters of the way, as they will rise while cooking.

5. Allow the muffins to cook until completely cooked through, about thirty minutes. Cool for a few minutes before enjoying.

# Blueberry Oatmeal Bread

The loaf is a simple and delicious way to enjoy your morning. When blueberries are in-season you can use fresh berries, but you can also choose to use frozen berries if they are what you have on hand. If you don't care for blueberries, try mixing things up and using blackberries or raspberries instead.

**The Servings:** 10

**The Time to Prepare/Cook:** 50 minutes

**The Calories:** 302

**The Sodium:** 26mg

**The Potassium:** 355mg

**The Ingredients:**

Eggs – 2

Soybean oil - .25 cup

Applesauce - .33 cup

Brown sugar - .5 cup

Skim milk - .75 cup

Cinnamon – 1 teaspoon

Low-sodium baking powder – 1 tablespoon

Rolled oats – 1 cup

White whole-wheat flour – 1 cup

All-purpose flour – 1.25 cup

Honey – 3 tablespoons

Blueberries – 1 cup

**The Instructions:**

1. Warm your oven to Fahrenheit 350 degrees and line a nine-by-five inch loaf pan with kitchen parchment.

2. In a medium bowl, whisk together the eggs with the brown sugar until completely combined. Stir in the skim milk, soybean oil, and applesauce.

3. In another bowl, combine the rolled oats, whole-wheat flour, all-purpose flour, cinnamon, and low-sodium baking powder. Once combined, stir the dry ingredients into the wet ingredients. Gently fold in the blueberries.

4. Pour the batter into the prepared baking pan and allow it to bake until cooked through, about thirty-five to forty-five minutes. Remove from the oven, and while still warm brush the top of the loaf with the honey. Once cool, cut the loaf and enjoy.

## Maple Banana Muffins

These muffins are a delicious addition to your day. You can easily make them ahead of time and then take them on-the-go when you have a busy morning or take them for a snack at work.

**The Servings:** 6

**The Time to Prepare/Cook:** 35 minutes

**The Calories:** 338

**The Sodium:** 30mg

**The Potassium:** 421mg

**The Ingredients:**

White whole-wheat flour – 1.75 cup

Cinnamon - .5 teaspoon

Rolled oats - .33 cup

Low-sodium baking powder – 1 teaspoon

Skim milk - .25 cup

Eggs, room temperature – 2

Maple syrup - .5 cup

Soybean oil - .33 cup

Vanilla extract – 1 teaspoon

Banana, mashed – 1 cup

**The Instructions:**

1. Preheat the oven to Fahrenheit 325 degrees and line twelve muffin cups with paper liners.

2. In a large bowl, whisk together the soybean oil and maple syrup until combined, and then stir in the eggs. Once fully combined, continue to stir in the mashed banana, skim milk, vanilla extract, low-sodium baking powder, and cinnamon. Lastly, stir in the flour. Be careful not to over mix the batter once the flour is added.

3. Divide the muffin batter between the prepared baking cups and set the pan in the center of the oven until fully cooked, about twenty-two to twenty-five minutes. Remove the muffins from the oven and allow them to cool for five minutes before transferring them from the pan to a wire cooling rack.

4. Enjoy the muffins warm or store them at room temperature for a couple of days, or in the fridge for up to five days.

## Waffles

These waffles are a great breakfast option, any day of the week! If you want waffles on the weekdays and don't have time to prepare them before work, then you can make them ahead of time and store them in the fridge or freezer.

**The Servings:** 5

**The Time to Prepare/Cook:** 20 minutes

**The Calories:** 360

**The Sodium:** 55mg

**The Potassium:** 610mg

**The Ingredients:**

Whole-wheat flour – 2 cups

Low-sodium baking powder – 4 teaspoons

Granulated sugar – 1 tablespoon

Soybean oil - .5 cup

Vanilla extract - .5 teaspoon

Skim milk – 1.75 cup

Eggs – 2

**The Instructions:**

1. Warm a waffle iron according to the manufacturer's directions while you prepare the waffles.

2. In a medium bowl, stir together the whole-wheat flour, low-sodium baking powder, and sugar.

3. In another bowl, whisk together the remaining ingredients. Once combined, stir the dry ingredients into the wet ingredients, just until combined. There may be some clumps, but that's okay. Don't over mix the batter.

4. Spray the waffle iron with a small amount of cooking spray and then add some batter to the hot iron. The amount of batter you add will depend on your specific waffle iron. Cook the waffles according to the manufacturer's directions until golden-brown. Remove from the iron and repeat the process until all of the waffles are cooked.

5. Enjoy with the toppings of your choice. Ideally, choose low-fat and low-sugar or sugar-free options. Fruit and sugar-free syrups or jams are a great choice.

# Breakfast Sausage Egg Casserole

This casserole is a great addition to your routine, as it makes the perfect weekend breakfast. However, you can easily enjoy it throughout the work week as well, if you prepare it ahead of time and store it in the fridge. Simply microwave a slice when you are ready for a delicious meal.

**The Servings:** 5

**The Time to Prepare/Cook:** 65 minutes

**The Calories:** 165

**The Sodium:** 284mg

**The Potassium:** 308mg

**The Ingredients:**

Egg Beaters egg whites – 1 cup

Egg – 1

Skim milk – 1.5 cups

Reduced-fat cheddar cheese, shredded – .5 cups

Turkey, ground – 5 ounces

White bread, low-sodium – 3 slices

Black pepper, ground - .75 teaspoon

Red pepper flakes - .5 teaspoon

Thyme, dried - .75 teaspoon

Apple juice – 3 tablespoons

**The Instructions:**

1. Start by warming the oven to Fahrenheit 350 degrees

and coating a nine-by-thirteen inch baking pan with non-stick cooking spray.

2. In a skillet, Add the ground turkey with the apple juice, thyme, red pepper flakes, and half of the black pepper. Cook until there is no pink remaining. If there is any excess fat, drain it off.

3. Slice the bread into cubes and sprinkle it evenly over the prepared baking pan. Add the cooked breakfast sausage and shredded cheese.

4. In a bowl, whisk together the egg, Egg beaters, skim milk, and remaining black pepper. Once combined, pour the egg mixture over the bread and breakfast sausage.

5. Cook the casserole until the eggs are fully cooked through, about forty to fifty minutes. Remove the pan from the oven and allow it to cool for a few minutes before serving.

## Pepper Scrambled Eggs in a Hole

These eggs take a spin off of the popular eggs in a toast hole. But, by using bell pepper instead of bread, not only are they healthier, they also get a delicious savory and sweet flavor. Enjoy them plain, or serve them with a little hot sauce for added flavor.

**The Servings:** 2

**The Time to Prepare/Cook:** 2

**The Calories:** 106

**The Sodium:** 120mg

**The Potassium:** 316mg

**The Ingredients:**

Eggs – 2

Egg whites – 2

Black pepper, ground - .25 teaspoon

Bell pepper, large – 1

**The Instructions:**

1. Slice the bell pepper in half width wise, so that it forms two round cups. Don't slice it from up to down, as you want to form rings with the bell pepper for the eggs to sit in. Remove the seeds from the bell pepper before slicing off the top stem and the very bottom of the pepper. Now, slice each half in half again. You should be left with four round rings of bell pepper.

2. Heat a large non-stick skillet over medium-high heat and spray it with non-stick spray. Place the rings into

the skillet and allow them to cook for minutes until they begin to brown. Flip the over and reduce the heat to medium.

3. Whisk together the eggs, egg whites, and black pepper and then divide the scrambled eggs between the four bell pepper rings. You want to pour the eggs into the center of the rings, so that they form and cook inside of the pepper rings.

4. Cover the pan with a lid and continue to cook the eggs for a couple minutes, until they are cooked to your preferred hardness. Remove from the heat and serve warm.

# Blueberry Pancakes Mix

This pancake mix is great to keep in the pantry, as it will allow you to make delicious blueberry pancakes at a moments notice! Although, you don't have to add blueberries. You can add any of your favorite healthy mix-ins, or just keep them plain.

**The Servings:** 3

**The Time to Prepare/Cook:** 12 minutes

**The Calories:** 261

**The Sodium:** 60mg

**The Potassium:** 709mg

**The Mix Ingredients:**

Low-sodium baking powder – 3 tablespoons

Sodium-free baking soda – 4 teaspoons

White whole-wheat flour – 5 cups

Brown sugar – 2 tablespoons

**The Pancake Ingredients:**

Egg – 1

Skim milk – 1 cup

Blueberries – 1 cup

Soybean oil – 1 tablespoon

Vanilla extract – 1 teaspoon

Pancake mix – 1 cup

**The Instructions:**

1. To make the mix, combine all of the mix ingredients together and store them in the pantry until you plan to use.

2. To create the pancakes, combine together all of the wet ingredients and then stir in the one cup of prepared pancake mix. Don't over work the batter, there may be lumps and that is okay. Gently fold in the blueberries.

3. Heat a non-stick skillet or griddle over medium heat. Once hot, grease with non-stick spray. Measure out your pancakes into evenly-sized rounds on the griddle and cook until the first side is golden. Gently flip the pancakes over and cook until the second side is golden. Remove from heat and cook any remaining batter.

4. Serve the pancakes warm with your favorite healthy toppings.

## Gluten-Free Pumpkin Pancakes

It's always great to have a delicious gluten-free recipe on hand, as wheat and gluten are two of the most common allergens. But, you can enjoy this recipe whether or not you have a gluten allergy, as it is always a great idea to vary your food consumption. Rather than always using wheat, you can use other grains and cereals as well, such as the sorghum flour used in this recipe.

**The Servings:** 3

**The Time to Prepare/Cook:** 20 minutes

**The Calories:** 232

**The Sodium:** 107

**The Potassium:** 465

**The Ingredients:**

Pumpkin puree - .5 cup

Egg whites – 4

Skim milk - .5 cup

Vanilla extract – 2 teaspoons

Brown sugar – 2 tablespoons

Cinnamon – 1 tablespoon

Low-sodium baking powder – 1 teaspoon

Xanthan gum - .25 teaspoon

Sweet white sorghum flour - .66 cup

**The Instructions:**

1. While you prepare the pancakes, allow a non-stick skillet or griddle over medium heat.

2. Begin by combining the baking powder, xanthan gum, cinnamon, brown sugar, and sorghum flour together in a bowl.

3. In another bowl, combine the pumpkin and egg whites together until they are completely combined. Stir in the vanilla and skim milk. Fold in the dry ingredients, being careful to not over work the batter. There may be some clumps, but as long as they are small it is okay.

4. Spray the griddle with non-stick skillet and then ladle the pancakes onto the hot service in evenly-sized rounds, about one-quarter of a cup each. Cook until the first side is golden brown, then flip over and cook the other side until the pancakes are fully cooked. Remove the pancakes from the heat, cook any remaining batter, and serve with your favorite healthy toppings.

## CHAPTER 4
## LUNCH AND DINNER ENTREES

The recipes in this chapter are great to provide you energy when you need it the most. There is a wide selection of choices, allowing you to easily customize what meal you eat based on your schedule for the day. You may choose to use a more quick meal when you are rushed or prepare a special dinner for you and your family. You may choose a dish that is lighter on the sodium or one with slightly more if you have been extra good and have a little leeway. You may choose an entree that is a full meal in one dish or you may choose one that is better complimented with a side dish. Whatever you want, you are sure to find what you need in this chapter.

### Taco Spaghetti Casserole

I your family can't decide on Italian or Tex-Mex for dinner, this casserole allows you to have the best of both worlds! Better yet, it is incredibly easy to cook, quick to make, and feeds a crowd. Enjoy it with a family and friends or make it for yourself and you can enjoy the leftovers for a week.

**The Servings:** 8

**The Time to Prepare/Cook:** 35 minutes

**The Calories:** 270

**The Sodium:** 376mg

**The Potassium:** 274mg

**The Ingredients:**

Whole-wheat spaghetti noodles - .8 ounces

Ground turkey, lean – 8 ounces

Water - .5 cup

Skim milk - .5 cup

Low-sodium chicken broth – 1 cup

All-purpose flour – 2 tablespoons

Extra virgin olive oil – 2 tablespoons

Monetary Jack cheese, low-fat, shredded – 1.5 cup

Diced tomatoes with green chilies – 10 ounces

Chili powder – 1 tablespoon

Cumin, ground – 1.5 tablespoon

Onion powder – 1 teaspoon

Garlic powder – 1 teaspoon

**The Instructions:**

1. Begin by setting the oven to Fahrenheit 350 degrees and preparing a nine-by-thirteen inch baking dish.

2. Boil a pot of water and then cook your spaghetti noodles until tender. Once cooked, drain off the water.

3. While the pasta cooks, work on the other aspects of your dish. Start by spray a skillet with non-stick cooking spray and add in the lean ground turkey. Cook until it is cooked through with no pink remaining, and then stir in the seasonings and water. Simmer the seasonings and meat together for five minutes, so that the seasonings and water creates a sauce around the meat.

4. Toss together the drained pasta, meat and seasonings, diced tomatoes, and half the Monterey Jack cheese in the pasta pot until the ingredients are fully combined. Spread the pasta mixture into the prepared baking dish and then sprinkle the remaining cheese over the top.

5. Cook the casserole in the oven until hot all the way through and the cheese on top is bubbly and gooey, about twenty minutes. Remove from the oven and serve immediately.

## Turkey Burgers

These burgers are full of flavor without the sodium! Enjoy them with a store-bought low-sodium bun, or a homemade bun for an extra special treat. You can even choose to wrap the burger in lettuce instead, if you are watching your weight. This burger is ideal, because it packs in flavor while still allowing you to use any of your favorite toppings.

**The Servings:** 8

**The Time to Prepare/Cook:** 15 minutes

**The Calories:** 93

**The Sodium:** 42mg

**The Potassium:** 189mg

**The Ingredients:**

Ground turkey, lean – 1 pound

Garlic cloves, minced – 3

Zucchini, shredded – 1.5 cups

Cumin, ground – 1 teaspoon

Onion powder – 1 teaspoon

Black pepper, ground - .25 teaspoon

**The Instructions:**

1. In a large bowl, use your hands to combine all of the ingredients together. You don't want to over work the meat, but you want to ensure the seasonings and zucchini are well distributed.

2. Divide the meat into six portions, and then form each portion between your hands into patties. Try pressing a thumb imprint into the top of the burgers, as this will help prevent any excess fat from running off.

3. At this point, you can cook the burgers, or you can freeze them on a baking sheet lined with anti-stick freeze paper. Once frozen, transfer them to a plastic bag and store in the freezer until use.

4. Cook the burgers in a skillet, under the oven's broiler, or on a grill until fully cooked through. This is poultry, so there should be no pink in the center of the patties, and a meat thermometer should show that the center temperature is at least Fahrenheit 165 degrees.

5. Serve the burgers with your favorite toppings and enjoy.

# Zucchini Turkey Taco Boats

These zucchini boats use the same method as a stuffed bell pepper or potato skin for a delicious and healthy dinner. Not only does it taste amazing, but by using a zucchini rather than a taco shell, you are able to cut down on sodium, increase nutrients, and watch your waistline.

**The Servings:** 4

**The Time to Prepare/Cook:** 65 minutes

**The Calories:** 187

**The Sodium:** 322mg

**The Potassium:** 847mg

**The Ingredients:**

Zucchini, medium – 4

Cumin – 1 teaspoon

Garlic powder – 1 teaspoon

Chili powder – 1 teaspoon

Paprika – 1 teaspoon

Ground turkey, lean – 8 ounces

Salsa, low-sodium - .5 cup

Water - .25 cup

Tomato sauce – 4 ounces

Onion, minced - .5 cup

Monetary Jack cheese, low-fat, shredded - .5 cup

**The Instructions:**

1. Start by preparing a large pot of boiling water, warming the oven to Fahrenheit 400 degrees, and preparing a nine-by-thirteen inch baking dish. Into the baking dish, pour the salsa and then set aside.

2. Slice the zucchini in half lengthwise and then use a small spoon to scoop out a small amount of the 'meat' of the squash. You don't want to remove all of the squash's meat, but only the center portion. Leave around one-quarter of an inch of the meat around the rim of the zucchini. Chop the zucchini that you removed into small pieces and set them aside for later use.

3. Add the zucchini to the prepared water and allow it to boil for one minute to often. Remove it from the water and then set aside.

4. Spray a large skillet with non-stick cooking spray and add in the ground turkey. Allow it to cook over medium heat until it is fully cooked with no pink remaining. Add in the chopped up zucchini pieces along with the

water, tomato sauce, and onion. Cover the skillet with a lid and allow it to simmer over low for twenty minutes.

5. Arrange the boiled zucchini shells in the prepared baking pan on top of the salsa. Once the skillet mixture is done cooking, remove it from the heat and stuff the zucchini shells with the mixture. Press the mixture firmly into the shells, so that it all fits and doesn't fall out. Sprinkle the top with cheese.

6. Cover the pan with aluminum foil and allow the dish to cook in the oven until fully cooked and the cheese is melted, about thirty minutes.

## Chicken Pineapple Kabobs

These kabobs are a treat, and will make you want to fire up the grill more often. Just because you have to watch your blood pressure doesn't mean you can't fit in at the family barbecue, too. You can enjoy these kabobs, turkey burgers, and low-sodium versions of all your traditional favorites.

**The Servings:** 8

**The Time to Prepare/Cook:** 25 minutes

**The Calories:** 227

**The Sodium:** 255mg

**The Potassium:** 577mg

**The Ingredients:**

Chicken breast, boneless and skinless, sliced into 2" pieces – 4

Low-sodium soy sauce – 3 tablespoons

Brown sugar – 3 tablespoons

Sesame seed oil – 1 tablespoon

Ginger, ground - .5 teaspoon

Garlic powder – 1 teaspoon

Pineapple chunks, drained – 20 ounces

Low-sodium barbecue sauce - .5 cup

**The Instructions:**

1. In a shallow glass dish whisk together the soy sauce, brown sugar, sesame seed oil, ginger, and garlic. Toss the chicken and pineapple in this mixture, cover the pan with some plastic wrap, and allow it to chill in the

fridge and marinate for at least two hours. You can make these up to twenty-four hours ahead of time and store them in the fridge until ready to cook.

2. Preheat your grill to a medium heat, oil the grates, and then stick the pineapple and chicken on skewers. Grill them until fully cooked through, turning occasionally, for about fifteen to twenty minutes. The chicken should reach an internal temperature of at least Fahrenheit 165 degrees.

# White Chicken Enchiladas

Most enchiladas are packed full of sodium upon more sodium. But, this twist on the classic brings you all the flavors you want, while also taking care of your heart.

**The Servings:** 8

**The Time to Prepare/Cook:** 40 minutes

**The Calories:** 303

**The Sodium:** 409mg

**The Potassium:** 377mg

**The Ingredients:**

Chicken breast, cooked and shredded – 2 cups

Monterey jack cheese, low-fat – 1.5 cups

Salsa, low-sodium - .5 cup

Chili powder – 1 teaspoon

Cumin, ground – 1 teaspoon

Extra virgin olive oil – 2 tablespoons

All-purpose flour – 2 tablespoons

Chicken broth, low-sodium – 2 cups

Green chilies, diced – 4 ounces

Black pepper, ground - .5 teaspoon

Sour cream, low-fat – 8 ounces

Whole-wheat tortillas, 6-inches – 8

Cilantro, fresh, chopped -.25 cup

**The Instructions:**

1. Preheat the oven to Fahrenheit 375 degrees and prepare a nine-by-thirteen inch baking dish.

2. In a bowl, toss together the shredded chicken, chili powder, half of the cumin, and the salsa. Once combined, divide the mixture between the tortillas, roll them up, and then place them in the prepared baking pan seam-side down. Set the pan to the side.

3. In a saucepan over medium heat combine the oil and flour. Allow them to cook for a minute or two while stirring, until the flour smells toasty and almost nutty. Slowly whisk in the chicken broth and allow it to warm up over medium-high until thickened, about six minutes. Stir in the green chilies, black pepper, remaining cumin, and one cup of cheese until melted.

4. Pour the prepared white enchilada sauce over the rolled enchiladas in the pan. Sprinkle the remaining half cup of cheese over the top. Allow the enchiladas to cook in the oven until heated through and the cheese has melted and bubbled up, about twenty-five minutes. Top with cilantro and enjoy.

# Pressure Cooker Red Beans and Rice

Red beans and rice are a flavorful Cajun classic, and this version is also vegan! You are able to get all the protein you need from the beans in this dish, along with a side of rice. Enjoy these red beans and rice as-written for a mild dish, or add in some low-sodium hot sauce and cayenne pepper to increase the spiciness level to your taste.

**The Servings:** 10

**The Time to Prepare/Cook:** 65 minutes

**The Calories:** 173

**The Sodium:** 15mg

**The Potassium:** 724mg

**The Ingredients:**

Red kidney beans, dried – 1 pound

Celery, sliced – 3 stalks

Bell pepper, diced – 1

Garlic, minced – 5 cloves

Onion, diced – 1

Bay leaves – 2

Black pepper, ground - .25 teaspoon

Cayenne pepper - .25 teaspoon

Oregano, dried – 1 teaspoon

Thyme, dried – 1 teaspoon

Paprika, smoked – 1 teaspoon

Water – 4 cups

**The Instructions:**

1. Wash the beans under cold water and remove any beans that are spoiled. Add them into the electric pressure cooker along with the remaining ingredients and give them a good stir.

2. Lock the lid of the pressure cooker and set it to high pressure for sixty minutes. Once it is done cooking, allow the pressure to naturally release for twenty minutes before opening the lid.

3. Serve the red beans with warm rice for a complete meal.

# Fettuccine Alfredo

This creamy and cheesy classic is made heart-healthy so that you can enjoy it to your heart's content! Enjoy it alone, or add in some of your favorite vegetables, chicken, or seafood for an extra special treat.

**The Servings:** 6

**The Time to Prepare/Cook:** 30 minutes

**The Calories:** 321

**The Sodium:** 43mg

**The Potassium:** 255mg

**The Ingredients:**

All-purpose flour – 2 tablespoons

Extra virgin olive oil – 1 tablespoon

Garlic, minced – 3 cloves

Chicken broth, low-sodium – 1 cup

Black pepper, ground - .25 teaspoon

Skim milk – 1 cup

Fettuccine noodles – 12 ounces

Parsley, chopped - .25 cup

Parmesan cheese, low-sodium - .75 cup

**The Instructions:**

1. In a skillet on medium heat the olive oil with the garlic until it is fragrant, about one minute. Stir in the flour to form a paste, allowing it to toast for a minute.

2. Quickly whisk in the chicken broth, using the whisk to break up any lumps that might form. Stir in the skim milk and then allow it to simmer until thickened, about seven minutes.

3. Meanwhile, boil a pot of water and cook the pasta until it is tender. Drain off the water and set the pasta aside.

4. Remove the sauce pot from the heat and stir in the Parmesan cheese and black pepper until the cheese is melted. Add in the cooked pasta and toss all of the ingredients together before serving.

# Pesto Spaghetti Squash 'Pasta'

This pasta is made with spaghetti squash, which gives it depth and a slight sweetness that pairs perfectly with the fresh pesto. Because it is made with squash instead of pasta, it also makes it healthier and lower in calories, ideal for those watching their weight.

**The Servings:** 4

**The Time to Prepare/Cook:** 45 minutes

**The Calories:** 300

**The Sodium:** 169mg

**The Potassium:** 1361mg

**The Ingredients:**

Spaghetti squash – 1

Bell pepper, diced – 1

Broccoli florets, chopped – 4 cups

Spinach – 6 cups

Garlic, minced – 6 cloves

Lemon juice – 2 tablespoons

Nutritional yeast - .33 cup

Basil, fresh – 1 cup

Silken tofu – 8 ounces

**The Instructions:**

1. Begin by setting the oven to Fahrenheit 400 degrees and preparing a baking sheet. Slice the spaghetti

squash in half lengthwise, use a large spoon to scoop out the seeds, and place both squash halves on the baking sheet. Allow the squash to roast in the oven until it is tender and a fork can easily run through it.

2. Meanwhile, steam the broccoli and bell pepper together until tender.

3. While the vegetables cook, make your pesto sauce by blending together the silken tofu, fresh basil, nutritional yeast, lemon juice, spinach, and garlic in the blender until completely smooth.

4. After the vegetables have been steamed add them into a large bowl. Then, take a fork and run it through both halves of the squash to create 'noodles.' place all of the squash noodles into the vegetable bowl and then pour in the pesto. Toss them all together until the vegetables are evenly coated. Serve alone, or with a little low-sodium Parmesan cheese over the top.

## Honey Lime Chicken

This is the perfect flavorful chicken to be served alongside your favorite side dishes from the next chapter. But, you can also use this chicken to create other dishes with more flavor. For instance, you may choose to eat this chicken with a salad for dinner one night, and then for lunch the next day you can turn it into a chicken salad sandwich.

**The Servings:** 8

**The Time to Prepare/Cook:** 25 minutes

**The Calories:** 90

**The Sodium:** 123mg

**The Potassium:** 229mg

**The Ingredients:**

Chicken breast, skinless and boneless, cut into 1" pieces – 1 pound

Cayenne pepper - .25 teaspoon

Lime juice – 2 tablespoons

Soy sauce, low-sodium – 1.5 tablespoons

Honey – 2 tablespoons

Garlic, minced – 3 cloves

Parsley, chopped - .25 cup

Lime, sliced - 1

**The Instructions:**

1. Warm the oven to Fahrenheit 400 degrees and line a

baking sheet with kitchen aluminum.

2. Toss all of the ingredients except for the parsley together in a bowl. Use your hands to fully massage the marinade into the chicken meat. Transfer the mixture to the prepared pan and cover it with a sheet of kitchen aluminum.

3. Roast the chicken until fully cooked with an internal temperature of at least Fahrenheit 165 degrees, about twenty minutes. Sprinkle the parsley over the top and serve.

# Roasted Carrot Soup

Whether you just want a comforting bowl of soup or a hearty soup and salad or sandwich combo, this cozy soup is a delicious addition to your repertoire. Try storing some in the freezer for quick last-minute meals, which will especially come in handy if you come down with a cold or the flu.

**The Servings:** 6

**The Time to Prepare/Cook:** 50 minutes

**The Calories:** 144

**The Sodium:** 106mg

**The Potassium:** 733mg

**The Ingredients:**

Carrots, peeled and cut into large pieces – 1.5 pounds

Garlic, peeled – 4 cloves

Onion, diced – 1

Extra virgin olive oil – 2 tablespoons

Basil, dried – 1 teaspoon

Black pepper, ground - .25 teaspoon

Cumin, ground – 1 teaspoon

Whole peeled tomatoes – 28 ounces

Greek yogurt, low-fat - .5 cup

**The Instructions:**

1. Warm the oven to Fahrenheit 400 degrees and coat two baking sheets with non-stick spray.

2. In a large bowl, toss together the garlic, onion, carrots, cumin, black pepper, and olive oil until evenly coated. Spread the vegetables on the baking sheets, being careful to not overcrowd them. Roast the vegetables until they are tender and browned, about thirty minutes, stirring them a few times during the cooking process. Allow the vegetables to cool for a few minutes.

3. While you allow the vegetables to cool, take the canned whole tomatoes and drain the liquid off into a measuring cup, setting it aside for later use.

4. Add half of your roasted vegetables into a blender or food processor along with half of the drained tomatoes. Puree the mixture until creamy and then pour it into the pot. Repeat this process with the remaining tomatoes and roasted vegetables.

5. Into your pot, stir the Green yogurt, drained tomato juice. Allow the soup to simmer for ten minutes until heated through, and serve warm.

## oli Stir-Fry

ir-fry you won't even miss the meat, as the of flavor from the sauce. Make sure that if ned chickpeas you buy ones without any added salt, as the sodium can increase rapidly if you use the wrong type of canned products.

**The Servings:** 4

**The Time to Prepare/Cook:** 17 minutes

**The Calories:** 284

**The Sodium:** 435mg

**The Potassium:** 741mg

**The Ingredients:**

Broccoli florets – 4 cups

Vegetable broth, low-sodium - .33 cup

Chickpeas, cooked – 2 cups

Garlic, minced – 5 cloves

Onion, diced – 1

Extra virgin olive oil – 1 tablespoon

Ginger, minced – 1 tablespoon

Onion powder – 1 teaspoon

Paprika – 1 teaspoon

Smoked paprika - .5 teaspoon

Black pepper, ground - .25 teaspoon

Cayenne pepper - .125 teaspoon

Honey – 2 tablespoon

Rice vinegar – 2 tablespoons

Soy sauce, low-sodium – 3 tablespoons

Water - .5 cup

Cornstarch – 1 tablespoon

**The Instructions:**

1. Add the olive oil to a large non-stick skillet or wok along with the spices, garlic, ginger, and onion. While stirring to prevent burning, saute until fragrant and tender, about three to four minutes.

2. Add the vegetable broth and broccoli florets to the wok, pan-frying until the broccoli is tender but still has a bit of bite left, about ten minutes. Do your best to not cook the broccoli too long, as you don't want mushy broccoli!

3. Meanwhile, in a bowl whisk together the soy sauce, honey, rice vinegar, water, and cornstarch to create a teriyaki sauce. Pour the sauce into the pan with the cooked broccoli, along with the chickpeas. Allow the dish to simmer for a few minutes, until the sauce has thickened. Serve alone or with rice.

# Pan-Seared Cod in White Wine Tomato Basil Sauce

This delicate cod is perfectly coated in a sweet and zesty sauce from the tomatoes and wine. Whether you are enjoying a dinner for one, a special date night, or a family dinner, everyone is sure to love this flavorful dish.

**The Servings:** 6

**The Time to Prepare/Cook:** 20 minutes

**The Calories:** 147

**The Sodium:** 347mg

**The Potassium:** 405mg

**The Ingredients:**

Cod fillets – 1.5 pounds

Extra virgin olive oil – 2 tablespoons

Cherry tomatoes, sliced in half – 2 cups

Garlic, minced – 3 cloves

Crushed red pepper flakes - .25 teaspoon

Basil, fresh, chopped - .5 cup

Lemon zest - .5 teaspoon

Lemon juice – 2 tablespoons

Black pepper, ground - .25 teaspoon

Dry white wine - .25 cup

**The Instructions:**

1. Begin by preparing the white wine tomato basil sauce. To do this, heat a saucepan over medium heat with the garlic and crushed red pepper flakes. Saute for just a minute while stirring until fragrant, being careful not to burn the spices.

2. Add the cherry tomatoes and allow them to saute while occasionally stirring until the skins are blistered and soft while still holding shape, about nine to twelve minutes. Stir in the white wine and bring the mixture to a light simmer before adding in the lemon juice, black pepper, basil, and lemon zest. Cook the sauce for two minutes before removing it from the heat, setting it aside for later.

3. Place a large non-stick skillet over medium heat and add in the oil, allowing it to warm. Meanwhile, pat the fish fillets dry with a clean kitchen towel, seasoning it with pepper. Place the cod in the warm oil and cook until browned, about three minutes. Flip the cod over gently, and cook the other side an additional three minutes until cooked through.

4. Pour the prepared white wine tomato basil sauce into the skillet with the cod and allow the two to cook and warm together for a minute before removing it from the heat and serving with your choice of sides.

# Creamy Mac and Cheese

Most macaroni and cheese is incredibly high is sodium, as cheese is naturally high in salt. But, you can now have a low-sodium version of your favorite comfort food! With the help of a few different dairy products and some nutritional yeast, which is regularly used for its cheese-like flavor, you can have one of your favorite dishes without any of the guilt.

**The Servings:** 3

**The Time to Prepare/Cook:** 20 minutes

**The Calories:** 458

**The Sodium:** 142mg

**The Potassium:** 378mg

**The Ingredients:**

Macaroni, dry – 7 ounces

Mustard, dry - .5 teaspoon

All-purpose flour – 2 tablespoons

Extra virgin olive oil – 2 tablespoons

Nutritional yeast – 2 tablespoons

Skim milk – 1 cup

Cream cheese, low-sodium – 1 ounce

Mozzarella, low-sodium, shredded – 1 ounce

Garlic powder - .25 teaspoon
Black pepper, ground - .25 teaspoon

**The Instructions:**

1. Boil a pot of water and cook the macaroni pasta until it is tender but still has a slight bite, and then drain off the water.

2. Meanwhile, prepare the cheese cause. In a saucepan over medium heat stir together the olive oil, all-purpose flour, garlic powder, dry mustard, and black pepper. Cook together until it is bubbly and warm with a slightly toasted smell. Be careful to not let the mixture burn.

3. Whisk in the milk a little at a time until it is fully incorporated without any lumps. This must be done slowly, rather than all at once. Allow the sauce to simmer for a minute, while constantly stirring, before adding in the cream cheese, mozzarella cheese, and nutritional yeast.

4. Allow the sauce to cook for a minute longer, until it is completed melted and combined. Remove from the heat, and toss together the pasta with the sauce before serving.

## Pulled Pork

Pulled pork is a great dish to keep in your freezer. Not only can you serve it alongside your favorite Southern sides or make a killer sandwich, you can add it to a number of dishes. Pasta, tacos, hash, casseroles, and more can all be improved with the addition of pulled pork. Just be sure that you use a lean cut of pork and low-sodium or sodium-free barbecue sauce. Check out Chapter Seven for a homemade barbecue sauce that will knock your socks off, or you can purchase Mrs. Taste Zero Sodium Barbecue Sauce online.

**The Servings:** 12

**The Time to Prepare/Cook:** 7 hours

**The Calories:** 278

**The Sodium:** 71mg

**The Potassium:** 516mg

**The Ingredients:**

Pork roast, fat trimmed off – 2 pounds

Barbecue sauce, low-sodium – .75 cups

Cinnamon - .125 teaspoon

Chili powder – .74 teaspoon

Cumin, ground - .125 teaspoon

Garlic cloves, minced – 2

Onion diced – .5

Brown sugar – .75 teaspoon

Water - .25 cup

**The Instructions:**

1. Into a crock-pot add your onion, garlic, and water. Set it aside.

2. In a small bowl, combine together the spices and brown sugar, and then rub them into the meat of the pork roast. Place the spiced roast in the crock pot on top of the onions, cover the pot with a lid, and cook the pork on low for six to eight hours. When the meat is done cooking, it will easily shred with a fork.

3. Remove the pork roast from the pot and shred it with a pair of forks. Once shredded, toss it with the barbecue sauce and a little of the cooking liquid from the crock-pot until it is well-coated. Place the roast back in the crock-pot, and cook it until for twenty minutes to an hour, until the flavors have melded. Enjoy with your choice of bread or sides.

## Turkey Chili

This chili can please a crowd, and nobody will even realize that it is completely heart-healthy! Enjoy this chili with your favorite low-sodium toppings, or you can even combine it with the Creamy Mac and Cheese for a cheesy creamy dish.

**The Servings:** 6

**The Time to Prepare/Cook:** 50 minutes

**The Calories:** 317

**The Sodium:** 287mg

**The Potassium:** 1046mg

**The Ingredients:**

Ground turkey, lean – 1 pound

Extra virgin olive oil – 2 teaspoons

Onion, diced – 1

Garlic, minced – 3 cloves

Red bell pepper, chopped – 1

Oregano, dried, ground – 1 teaspoon

Cumin, ground – 2 teaspoons

Chili powder – 4 tablespoons

Cayenne pepper - .25 teaspoon

Corn kernels – 2 cups

Kidney beans, cooked – 2 cups

Diced tomatoes – 28 ounces

Chicken broth, low-sodium – 1.25 cup

**The Instructions:**

1. In a large pot over medium-high, cook your onion, bell pepper, garlic, and the olive oil until tender, about five minutes.

2. Add in the meat and continue to cook until it is cooked through and no longer pink, then stir in all of the seasonings. Saute for an additional thirty seconds while stirring so the flavors meld.

3. Stir in the kidney beans, tomatoes, corn, and chicken broth. Bring the mixture to a boil and then reduce to a simmer, allowing it to simmer over medium-low for thirty to forty-five minutes, until flavorful. Serve with your favorite toppings.

## Italian Chicken and Vegetables

This roasted dish is incredibly quick to assemble and cook, making it a great go-to option when you are busy with little time on your hands. Try to keep these ingredients on hand, and you will feel good knowing that no matter what comes up in life, you always have what you need to prepare a delicious and heart-healthy dinner.

**The Servings:** 8

**The Time to Prepare/Cook:** 35 minutes

**The Calories:** 202

**The Sodium:** 171mg

**The Potassium:** 697mg

**The Ingredients:**

Chicken breasts, boneless and skinless – 4

Zucchini, sliced – 1

Basil, dried – 1 tablespoon

Cherry tomatoes, sliced in half – 1 cup

Bell pepper, cut into strips – 1

Mushrooms, sliced – 1 cup

Mozzarella cheese, low-sodium, shredded – 1 cup

**The Instructions:**

1. Warm the oven to Fahrenheit 375 degrees and prepare a casserole dish.

2. Place the chicken into the casserole dish and sprinkle

the basil, tomatoes, zucchini, bell peppers, and rooms over the top. Lastly, sprinkle over the ch

3. Roast the dish until the chicken is cooked through with an internal temperature of at least Fahrenheit 165 degrees and then remove it from the oven, about twenty-five to thirty minutes. Allow the chicken to rest for ten to fifteen minutes before slicing and serving.

## Tex Mex Chicken and Zucchini

This dish only takes a few minutes to prepare and you can cook it all in one skillet, making it a flavorful and super easy dish. Top it with some of your favorite heart-healthy taco ingredients, such as light sour cream, for an extra treat.

**The Servings:** 8

**The Time to Prepare/Cook:** 25 minutes

**The Calories:** 257

**The Sodium:** 207

**The Potassium:** 808

**The Ingredients:**

Zucchini, diced – 1

Corn kernels – 1 cup

Garlic, minced – 3 cloves

Bell pepper, diced – 2

Onion, diced – 1

Extra virgin olive oil – 1 tablespoon

Chicken breast, boneless and skinless, cut into 1" pieces – 1 pound

Black beans, cooked – 2 cups

Tomatoes, diced – 2 cups

Cumin, ground – 1.5 tablespoons

Chili powder – 2 tablespoons

Onion powder – 1 teaspoon

Garlic powder – 1 teaspoon

Black pepper, ground - .25 teaspoon

Cilantro, chopped - .5 cup

Green onions, chopped - .5 cup

Monterey jack, low-fat – 1 cup

**The Instructions:**

1. Warm a large skillet over medium heat and then add in the olive oil, garlic, onion, and bell pepper, allowing the vegetables to saute together for three minutes.

2. Use a spatula to scoot the vegetables over to the side of the skillet and then add the black pepper, cumin, and chicken to the center of the skillet. Cook the chicken for about five minutes, giving it an occasional stir.

3. Stir the remaining seasonings into the skillet along with the tomatoes, corn, zucchini, and black beans. Reduce the heat to medium-low, cover the skillet with a lid, and allow the skillet to simmer for ten minutes.

4. Top the skillet with the cheese and cover with the lid again, until the cheese melts. Once melted, top the skillet with the cilantro and green onions, and serve alone or with your choice of sides.

## Turkey Meatloaf

This turkey meatloaf will bring back the flavor of home. Enjoy it with all of your favorite sides and then make comforting meatloaf sandwiches with the leftovers. Just remember to use low-sodium ketchup, as any pre-made products such as that will be high in sodium if you don't purchase the heart-healthy varieties.

**The Servings:** 8

**The Time to Prepare/Cook:** 70 minutes

**The Calories:** 113

**The Sodium:** 58

**The Potassium:** 180

**The Ingredients:**

Egg – 1

Balsamic vinegar – 2 tablespoons

Red pepper flakes - .25 teaspoon

Thyme, dried - .5 teaspoon

Rosemary, dried - .5 teaspoon

Basil, dried - .5 teaspoon

Oregano, dried - .5 teaspoon

Garlic cloves, minced – 1 tablespoon

Onion, diced - .5

Ground turkey, low-fat – 1 pound

Breadcrumbs, low-sodium - .5 cup

Ketchup, no salt-added - .25 cup, plus 2 tablespoons

**The Instructions:**

1. Warm the oven to Fahrenheit 375 degrees and prepare a nine-by-five inch loaf pan for the meatloaf with non-stick cooking spray.

2. In a skillet, saute the onion until they are nearly transparent, about five minutes. Stir in the garlic and cook for one additional minute, until fragrant.

3. Add the vegetables and all the remaining ingredients except for two tablespoons of the ketchup to a large bowl. Use your hands to incorporate the mixture evenly. Pour the mixture into the prepared loaf pan and smooth it out with your hands or a spatula. You want to even out the top and ensure there are no air pockets in the center.

4. Spread the remaining two tablespoons of ketchup over the top of the meatloaf and bake it until cooked through with an internal temperature of Fahrenheit 165 degrees, about fifty to sixty minutes. Allow the loaf to sit for a few minutes before slicing and serving.

# Hamburger Goulash

This traditional American comfort food is quick and easy to prepare while also being hearty and satisfying. Feel free to make your own adjustments and changes to the dish, such as adding mushrooms or potatoes. Goulash has many different variations, and you are free to add your own, just make sure that they are low-sodium and heart-healthy!

**The Servings:** 6

**The Time to Prepare/Cook:** 30 minutes

**The Calories:** 331

**The Sodium:** 77mg

**The Potassium:** 970mg

**The Ingredients:**

Ground turkey, learn – 1 pound

Whole-wheat macaroni – 8 ounces

Bell pepper, diced – 1

Onion, diced – 1

Extra virgin olive oil – 2 teaspoons

Tomato sauce, low-sodium – 20 ounces

Diced tomatoes, low-sodium – 28 ounces

Black pepper, ground - .25 teaspoon

Cinnamon, ground – .125 teaspoon

**The Instructions:**

1. Boil a pot of water and cook the macaroni in it until tender, and then drain off the excess water.

2. Meanwhile, add the olive oil, ground turkey, onion, bell pepper, black pepper, and cinnamon into a large skillet. Brown together until the turkey is cooked through all the way and the onion and bell pepper are tender, about eight minutes.

3. Stir in the tomato sauce and diced tomatoes, stirring together until the tomatoes are heated through and simmering. Remove from the heat and stir in the pasta until the dish is completely combined. Serve warm.

## Cabbage, Potato, and White Bean Soup

Perfect for a cozy and satisfying soup on a cold evening, a simple meal to prepare in the crock-pot or pressure cooker, or even a soup you can make when trying to watch your wallet, the soup is a delicious and all-purpose meal that can serve you well.

**The Servings:** 6

**The Time to Prepare/Cook:** 40 minutes

**The Calories:** 306

**The Sodium:** 174mg

**The Potassium:** 1296mg

**The Ingredients:**

Vegetable broth, low-sodium – 6 cups

Diced tomatoes, low-sodium – 15 ounces

Yukon gold potatoes, diced – 1 pound

Cabbage, sliced - .5 head

White beans, cooked – 3 cups

Carrots, diced – 2

Celery, diced – 2 stalks

Leeks, sliced – 2

Garlic, minced – 3 cloves

Extra virgin olive oil – 2 tablespoons

Herbs de Provence, salt-free herbal seasoning – 1 tablespoon

Black pepper, ground - .25 teaspoon

Parsley, fresh, chopped - .25 cup

**The Instructions:**

1. After slicing the leeks allow them to soak in a bowl of water for ten minutes. Work them through your hands to separate the leek layers from each other, which will help to get any hidden dirt or sand out. Strain them out through a colander and run a little fresh water over them.

2. Add the leeks, celery, carrots, and olive oil to a large pot over medium-high heat and saute them for five minutes. Add in the garlic, herbs, and spices and then saute for one more minute until fragrant.

3. Stir in the beans, cabbage, potatoes, tomatoes, and vegetable broth. Bring the soup to a boil, reduce the heat to low, and cover with a lid, allowing all of the ingredients to simmer together for thirty minutes until tender. Serve alone, with crusty whole-wheat bread, or your choice of sides.

# Sloppy Joes

This quick and flavorful childhood favorite is a great option. Serve it alone, or alongside any of your favorite side dishes from this book. Cook it on the stove, or after assembling put it in a slow cooker on low heat for a few hours for an easy meal to come home to.

**The Servings:** 8

**The Time to Prepare/Cook:** 25 minutes

**The Calories:** 198

**The Sodium:** 143mg

**The Potassium:** 403mg

**The Ingredients:**

Ground turkey, lean – 1.5 pounds

Garlic powder – 1 teaspoon

Onion, diced – 1

Bell pepper, diced – 1

Ketchup, low-sodium – 1 cup

White vinegar – 3 tablespoons

Yellow mustard – 2 tablespoons

Worcestershire sauce – 1 tablespoon

Chili powder – 1 teaspoon

Brown sugar – 2 tablespoons

**The Instructions:**

1. In a large pot saute the onion and bell pepper for four minutes, until the onion is almost tender. Add in the ground turkey and brown until fully cooked and no pink is remaining, about seven to eight minutes.

2. Stir in the remaining ingredients and allow the mixture to simmer over medium heat until all the flavors have simmered together, about ten minutes. Serve over your favorite whole-wheat and low-sodium buns.

# eamy Tomato and Spinach Pasta

This pasta dish perfectly combines a zesty tomato sauce with creamy and indulgent Parmesan and cream cheese, which is then accentuated with the slightly bitter spinach. You will love the melody of flavors. Whether you are looking for a quick dinner or an easy lunch you can make ahead of time and store in the fridge until ready to serve, you are sure to love this dish.

**The Servings:** 4

**The Time to Prepare/Cook:** 25 minutes

**The Calories:** 336

**The Sodium:** 152mg

**The Potassium:** 792mg

**The Ingredients:**

Penne pasta, whole-wheat – 8 ounces

Extra virgin olive oil – 1 tablespoon

Garlic, minced – 2 cloves

Onion, diced – 1

Diced tomatoes, low-sodium – 15 ounces

Tomato paste, low-sodium – 2 tablespoons

Crushed red pepper flakes - .25 teaspoon

Basil, dried - .5 teaspoon

Oregano, dried - .5 teaspoon

Black pepper, ground - .25 teaspoon

Cream cheese, low-fat – 2 ounces

Parmesan, shredded, low-fat - .25 cup

Spinach – 4 ounces

Water - .5 cup

**The Instructions:**

1. Boil a pot of water and cook the penne in it until tender, and then drain off the excess water.

2. Meanwhile, prepare the sauce. Add the onion, garlic, and olive oil to a skillet over medium heat, sauteing until translucent and fragrant, about four minutes.

3. Stir the crushed red pepper, basil, oregano, pepper, diced tomatoes, tomato paste, and water into the pot, mixing until the tomato paste has dissolved. Reduce the heat to low and stir in the cream cheese, stirring until it has completely melted and made the sauce creamy. Stir in the Parmesan until melted.

4. Add the spinach to the sauce and allow it to cook until wilted, about two to three minutes. Once wilted, add in the cooked pasta and toss to coat it completely in the sauce. Serve warm.

# CHAPTER 5

# SIDE DISHES

It is easy to create side dishes for your meals. There are a wide variety of whole grains, bread, and salads you can prepare. However, these are not your only options. When it comes to side dishes, the options are limitless. In this chapter, I will give you some of my favorite side dishes that will bring flavor and variety to your DASH diet.

## Wild Rice and Mushroom Pilaf

You can certainly enjoy a simple bowl of brown rice with your meal, however, if you want something a little more exciting, try this pilaf made with wild rice and mushrooms for an extra savory and decadent flavor. It has white wine, but if you don't have any on hand you can use a little extra vegetable broth, instead.

**The Servings:** 8

**The Time to Prepare/Cook:** 90 minutes

**The Calories:** 228

**The Sodium:** 281

**The Potassium:** 404

**The Ingredients:**

Olive oil, divided – 3 tablespoons

Vegetable broth, low-sodium – 4 cups

Wild rice blend – 2 cups

Black pepper, ground - .25 teaspoon

Onion, diced – 1

Mushrooms, mixed, sliced – 1 pound

White wine, dry - .33 cup

Chives, chopped – 2 tablespoons

**The Instructions:**

1. Add one tablespoon of the olive oil to a large saucepan along with the onion and allow it to saute until tender, about five minutes over medium heat. Stir in the wild rice, and allow it to toast for thirty seconds while stirring.

2. Stir the vegetable broth into the rice, cover the pot with a lid, and allow it to simmer over low heat until all of the broth is absorbed by the rice, about forty-five minutes.

3. Meanwhile, add the remaining olive oil and mushrooms into a large skillet and saute them until browned, about eight minutes. Stir in the wine, and cook until it has evaporated, an additional four minutes.

4. Fluff the cooked rice with a fork and stir in the mushrooms and chives, then serve.

## Broccoli Gratin

Gratin is a delicious dish made with a creamy
This gratin makes use of broccoli and a topping of
breadcrumbs for a crunchy texture. Enjoy this dish to create
the ultimate comfort meal.

**The Servings:** 6

**The Time to Prepare/Cook:** 40 minutes

**The Calories:** 213

**The Sodium:** 239mg

**The Potassium:** 349mg

**The Ingredients:**

Broccoli florets – 5 cups

All-purpose flour – 2 tablespoons

Extra virgin olive oil - .25 cup

Half-n-half, fat-free – 1 cup

Garlic powder - .5 teaspoon

Cheddar cheese, low-fat, shredded – 1 cup

Black pepper, ground - .25 teaspoon

Panko bread crumbs - .75 cup

**The Instructions:**

1. Begin by warming the oven to Fahrenheit 350 degrees and prepare a nine-by-thirteen inch baking dish.

2. Boil a pot of water and lightly boil the broccoli florets for two minutes. Keep in mind, you don't want to

cook them very much, as you will continue to cook them in the oven. This is only to ensure they reach optimal texture. You can skip this step completely if you want your broccoli to have a bit more crunch to it.

3. In a saucepan, mix together the olive oil and flour and stir over medium until the flour smells toasty, stirring completely. Be careful not to burn the mixture. Stir in the half-n-half and the cheddar cheese until the cheese is melted and smooth. Lastly, stir in the black pepper.

4. Add the boiled broccoli to the baking dish along with the cheese sauce, and toss them together to coat. Spread the mixture into all crevices of the pan and sprinkle the panko over the top. Bake the gratin until golden brown, about fifteen to twenty minutes, and then serve.

# California Vegetables with Parmesan Bread Crumbs

This mix of California vegetables—including cauliflower, broccoli, and carrots—are coated in a delicious and crunchy blend of Parmesan cheese and Panko bread crumbs, with just a bit of cayenne pepper for spice. Enjoy these fresh out of the oven for a crunchy and tasty treat.

**The Servings:** 8

**The Time to Prepare/Cook:** 55 minutes

**The Calories:** 75

**The Sodium:** 47mg

**The Potassium:** 260mg

**The Ingredients:**

Cauliflower florets – 2 cups

Broccoli florets – 2 cups

Carrots, sliced – 2 cups

Extra virgin olive oil – 2 tablespoons

Parmesan cheese, low-sodium, shredded - .25 cup

Cayenne pepper, ground - .125 teaspoon

Panko bread crumbs - .25 cup

**The Instructions:**

1. Warm the oven to Fahrenheit 350 degrees and prepare a medium-sized baking dish for the vegetables.

2. In a bowl, toss together the vegetables with the olive

oil until they are fully and evenly coated. In a separate side bowl, toss together the cayenne pepper, Parmesan cheese, and panko bread crumbs. Once combined, add this mixture to the vegetables and toss until the vegetables are once again fully coated.

3. Pour the vegetables and any extra breadcrumbs into the prepared baking dish, cover with foil, and roast in the oven for thirty minutes. Now, remove the oven and roast for an additional fifteen minutes until crispy yet fork-tender.

# Rosemary and Parmesan Roasted Sweet Potatoes

The rosemary, garlic, and Parmesan offer the perfect savory umami flavor to pair with the natural sweetness of the orange sweet potato. This is a great side dish to keep on hand in the fridge, which you can then reheat to pair with nearly any meal.

**The Servings:** 6

**The Time to Prepare/Cook:** 40 minutes

**The Calories:** 190

**The Sodium:** 86

**The Potassium:** 521

**The Ingredients:**

Sweet potatoes, peeled, sliced into 1" pieces – 2 pounds

Garlic powder - .5 teaspoon

Extra virgin olive oil – 2 tablespoons

Rosemary, fresh, chopped – 1 tablespoon

Black pepper, ground - .25 teaspoon

Parmesan cheese, low-sodium, shredded - .25 cup

**The Instructions:**

1. Warm the oven to Fahrenheit 425 degrees and prepare a baking sheet by spreading kitchen parchment or aluminum on it to prevent sticking.
2. Place the prepared sweet potatoes onto the prepared baking sheet and toss them with half of the rosemary

along with the garlic powder, black pepper, and olive oil. Spread the mixture out evenly over the pan, and roast until golden-brown and tender, about twenty-five to thirty minutes.

3. Remove the potatoes from the oven, toss them with the remaining rosemary, and allow them to cool for five minutes. Now, toss them with the Parmesan and serve.

## Balsamic Spinach and Mushrooms

Mushrooms and balsamic both have natural umami qualities, which give them a deep savory flavor only found in a handful of foods. This flavor is irritable, especially on a diet in which your sodium is limited. Keep this side dish on hand and you will not only have a delicious meal component, but plenty of heart-healthy nutrients, as well.

**The Servings:** 4

**The Time to Prepare/Cook:** 22 minutes

**The Calories:** 83

**The Sodium:** 61

**The Potassium:** 598

**The Ingredients:**

Onion powder - .5 teaspoon

Garlic, minced – 4 cloves

Extra virgin olive oil – 1.5 tablespoons

Black pepper, ground - .25 teaspoon

Balsamic vinegar – 1 tablespoon

Mushrooms, sliced – 8 ounces

Baby spinach – 10 ounces

**The Instructions:**

1. In a large skillet over medium heat add the olive oil and mushrooms. Allow them to saute until browned, about eight to ten minutes while occasionally stirring. Stir in the garlic and the onion powder, cooking for an

additional one to two minutes until fragrant. Be careful to avoid burning.

2. Add in the spinach and continue stirring the skillet around so that the spinach can wilt evenly. Once the spinach is almost completely wilted, stir in the balsamic vinegar and then remove from the heat before serving.

## Smashed Brussels Sprouts

By smashing the Brussels sprouts before you roast them, the entire vegetable can absorb the flavor of the seasonings, giving you the best Brussels sprouts you have ever tasted. Feel free to adjust the seasonings to fit your preference, but you are sure to find that making them according them to the recipe is just as delicious.

**The Servings:** 6

**The Time to Prepare/Cook:** 55 minutes

**The Calories:** 179

**The Sodium:** 48

**The Potassium:** 639

**The Ingredients:**

Garlic, minced – 3 cloves

Extra virgin olive oil – 3 tablespoons

Brussels sprouts – 2 pounds

Black pepper, ground - .5 teaspoon

Balsamic vinegar – 2 tablespoons

Leek, sliced – 1

Parmesan cheese, low-sodium, shredded - .5 cup

**The Instructions:**

1. Warm the oven to Fahrenheit 450 degrees and prepare one or two large baking sheets with kitchen parchment.

2. Remove the stems from the Brussels sprouts and any

yellowed leaves, but leaving the sprouts whole. Steam the sprouts on the stove until tender, about twenty to twenty five minutes. Drain off the water once they are cooked.

3. Meanwhile, in a bowl whisk together the balsamic vinegar, olive oil, black pepper, and minced garlic. Toss the seasoned oil with the steamed Brussels sprouts and the sliced leak, spreading it out on the prepared baking sheet(s).

4. Take a glass or a jar and gently press down on the top of each of the Brussels sprouts until they have all formed flat patties. Sprinkle the Parmesan cheese over the top.

5. Roast the Brussels sprouts until golden-brown and crispy, about fifteen minutes, and then serve while still warm.

## Mediterranean Chickpea Salad

This chickpea salad packs a punch of fresh flavor from mint, parsley, lemon, and more. You can also get a host of nutrients that will keep you energized and satisfied on even the most busy of days. Prepare this salad ahead of time and store it in the fridge, so that it is ready when you need it the most.

**The Servings:** 4

**The Time to Prepare/Cook:** 20 minutes

**The Calories:** 386

**The Sodium:** 50mg

**The Potassium:** 1060mg

**The Ingredients:**

Chickpeas, cooked – 4 cups

Bell pepper, diced – 1

English cucumber, diced – 4

Tomatoes, diced – 2

Red onion, diced - .5

Parsley, fresh, chopped - .5 cup

Mint, fresh, chopped - .5 cup

Lemon juice – 2 tablespoons

Extra virgin olive oil – 2 tablespoons

Black pepper, ground - .5 teaspoon

Paprika, ground – 1 teaspoon

**The Instructions:**

1. If you are using canned chickpeas, be sure that they are low-sodium. Also, strain them through a sieve and run them under cold water to remove as much sodium as possible. Add the rinsed chickpeas to a bowl along with the olive oil, lemon juice, and paprika, tossing them together. Place the chickpeas in a bowl for at least fifteen minutes or up to an hour to marinade.

2. Once marinated, toss in the onion, bell pepper, cucumbers, tomatoes, parsley, mint, and black pepper. Taste and adjust the seasoning to your preference. Serve immediately, or store in the fridge for up to three days.

## Thai Veggie 'Noodle' Salad

This salad uses a vegetable spiralizer to create noodles for a fun and interesting texture. While you could simply chop up all the vegetables, you will be missing out on the unique texture this salad has to offer. If you don't currently have a vegetable spiralizer, they are now quite easy and affordable to purchase at nearly any grocery store and online.

**The Servings:** 4

**The Time to Prepare/Cook:** 15 minutes

**The Calories:** 323

**The Sodium:** 43mg

**The Potassium:** 606mg

**The Ingredients:**

Chickpeas, cooked – 2 cups

English cucumber, spiralized - .5

English cucumber, diced - .5

Bell pepper, diced – 1 cup

Onion, diced - .25 cup

Carrots, diced – 3

Cilantro, chopped - .5 cup

Garlic, minced - .5 teaspoon

Dill, fresh, chopped – 2 tablespoons

Garlic powder - .125 teaspoon

White vinegar – 2 tablespoons

Extra virgin olive oil – 3 tablespoons

Lemon juice – 3 tablespoons

Chia seeds - .5 tablespoon

Sesame seeds - .5 tablespoons

Rice vinegar – 2 tablespoons

Honey – 2 tablespoons

**The Instructions:**

1. In a bowl, whisk together the garlic, dill, white vinegar, lemon juice, olive oil, and garlic powder until it emulsifies into a smooth vinaigrette. Add the cucumber, carrot, cilantro, bell pepper, onion, and chickpeas to the bowl, tossing them to coat. You can now either move onto the next step or allow the salad to marinade for a little while for a stronger flavor.

2. In a small bowl, whisk together the rice vinegar, honey, chia seeds, and sesame seeds. Once combined, pour this mixture over the prepared salad and serve.

# Green Cabbage Cucumber Salad

This is a great salad that you can make ahead and store in the fridge to enjoy at any point, as it won't wilt. You can make it up to three days ahead of time, and the longer you store it in the fridge the more flavorful it will become from marinating.

**The Servings:** 6

**The Time to Prepare/Cook:** 15 minutes

**The Calories:** 195

**The Sodium:** 55mg

**The Potassium:** 618

**The Ingredients:**

Green cabbage, shredded – 1

Cucumbers, thinly sliced – 3

Green onions, thinly sliced – 4

Dill, fresh, chopped – 2 tablespoons

Extra virgin olive oil – 6 tablespoons

Distilled white vinegar – 4 tablespoons

Black pepper, ground - .25 teaspoon

**The Instructions:**

1. In a bowl, whisk together the olive oil, white vinegar, and black pepper until combined. Add the vegetables to the bowl and toss until they are fully coated. Taste test the salad and adjust the seasoning to your preference.

2. Serve the salad immediately, or store it in the fridge until you are ready to serve.

# Lebanese Spicy Potatoes

These potatoes are spicy, crispy, and irresistible. However, if you want a similar effect but don't like spicy dishes, then you can use smoked paprika instead of red pepper flakes. This will give the potatoes a flavor that is a mix of smokey, sweet, and savory rather than spicy. However you choose to make these potatoes, you are sure to love them!

**The Servings:** 8

**The Time to Prepare/Cook:** 35 minutes

**The Calories:** 318

**The Sodium:** 23mg

**The Potassium:** 1579

**The Ingredients:**

Yukon gold potatoes, cubed – 8

Garlic, minced – 3 cloves

Extra virgin olive oil, divided – 2 tablespoons

Cilantro, chopped – 1 cup

Red pepper flakes, divided – 2 teaspoons

Black pepper, ground - .25 teaspoon

**The Instructions:**

1. Warm the oven to Fahrenheit 450 degrees and line a baking sheet with kitchen parchment. Pour the cubed potatoes onto the baking pan along with one tablespoon of the olive oil, tossing them until fully coated. Roast the potatoes until golden-brown and crispy, about thirty minutes. You should flip the potatoes over halfway through the cooking time.

2. Meanwhile, add the remaining olive oil, garlic, and half of both the cilantro and red pepper to a skillet. Allow them to saute together over medium heat until the garlic is golden, being careful to not burn it, about one minute. Remove the oil from the heat.

3. Once the potatoes are done cooking, transfer them to a large bowl and toss them with the oil mixture along with the remaining red pepper flakes and cilantro. Serve hot and alone or with a garnish of lemon.

## Green Beans with Garlic and Onions

These green beans have a delicious sweet and savory flavor from the garlic and onions, which are then complemented with the nutty toasted almonds and warm spices. You can easily prepare this dish ahead of time, and store it in the fridge until you are ready to reheat and enjoy.

**The Servings:** 4

**The Time to Prepare/Cook:** 30 minutes

**The Calories:** 122

**The Sodium:** 17mg

**The Potassium:** 514

**The Ingredients:**

Garlic, minced – 3 cloves

Yellow onion – 1

Honey – 1 teaspoon

Vegetable broth, low-sodium, divided - .75 cup

Thyme, fresh – 2 teaspoons

Black pepper, ground - .25 teaspoon

Green beans, trimmed – 1.5 pounds

Silvered almonds, toasted - .25 cup

**The Instructions:**

1. Add two tablespoons of the vegetable broth to a large skillet along with the onion and allow the onions to saute until they are lightly caramelized and golden-

brown, about ten minutes over medium-low heat. As the vegetable broth evaporates, you can add additional broth one tablespoon at a time. Be careful not to drown the onions in broth. Stir in the honey and thyme, and cook for two additional minutes, until fragrant.

2. Into the skillet add the minced garlic, green beans, black pepper, and a little more vegetable broth. Cover the pan with a lid and steam the green beans until tender, about seven to eight minutes. While they cook, lift the lid every few minutes to give the beans a good stir and add any extra broth, if the pan becomes dry. Once done, the beans will be tender and the onions will be dark brown.

3. Remove the lid off of the skillet and continue cooking until the pan is dry without any extra broth. Sprinkle the toasted almonds over the top and remove the pan from the heat before serving.

## Honey Thyme Glazed Carrots

The honey and thyme pair together perfectly to create a deep sweet and savory flavor quite unique. Unlike other ingredients, the honey offers a unique flavor with its sweetness and thyme has a woody flavor that pairs with it perfectly. These carrots pair well with nearly any dish, and are easy to keep on hand to enjoy on a regular basis.

**The Servings:** 6

**The Time to Prepare/Cook:** 20 minutes

**The Calories:** 211

**The Sodium:** 105mg

**The Potassium:** 495mg

**The Ingredients:**

Carrots, peeled and sliced – 2 pounds

Extra virgin olive oil - .33 cup

Honey - .25 cup

Thyme, fresh – 1 tablespoon

Black pepper, ground - .25 teaspoon

**The Instructions:**

1. Warm the oven to Fahrenheit 400 degrees and prepare a glass baking dish.
2. Add the carrots, oil, honey, and seasonings to the dish, tossing them together until the carrots are fully and evenly coated in the mixture.
3. Place the pan in the oven and roast until the carrots are

tender, about twenty minutes. You should stir them halfway through the cooking process, so that they roast evenly. Serve while warm.

# Maple Roasted Beets and Carrots

Beets and carrots are a match made in heaven, which is made even better with the sweet and spicy maple black pepper dressing. You only need a handful of ingredients to prepare this delicious side dish, but it is fancy enough to serve alongside even an elaborate date night meal.

**The Servings:** 6

**The Time to Prepare/Cook:** 35 minutes

**The Calories:** 154

**The Sodium:** 85mg

**The Potassium:** 393mg

**The Ingredients:**

Beets, peeled and diced – 4

Carrots, peeled and sliced – 5

Black pepper, ground - .25 teaspoon

Extra virgin olive oil – .25 cup

Maple syrup – 3 tablespoons

**The Instructions:**

1. Warm the oven to Fahrenheit 425 degrees, center the oven's rack, and prepare a large baking sheet by coating it with kitchen parchment.

2. Add all of the ingredients onto the baking sheet, and toss them together until they are evenly and fully coated in the sweet glaze.

3. Roast the vegetables until tender, about fifteen to thir-

ty minutes, depending on the size you slice them. It is best to stir them once halfway through the cooking process, so that they roast evenly.

4. Remove the dish from the oven and allow it to cool just a minute before serving. You can serve these as their own side dish or you can use them as a topping for extravagant salads.

# CHAPTER 6
# SNACKS

Snacks are a great addition to the DASH diet, as they allow you to boost your energy through calories and nutrients, as needed. If you are going to be especially busy, it is a good idea to keep these snacks prepared ahead of time, so that you can simply grab them and go. This will allow you to enjoy snacks whether you are at home, the office, or running errands. You will find a variety of snacks in this chapter, to fit all your snacking needs.

# Baked Sweet Potato Chips

These chips are sweet and savory with a slight spicy and smokey flavor from the chili powder. Feel free to change up the sodium-free seasoning options to create new flavors and combos.

**The Servings:** 4

**The Time to Prepare/Cook:** 30 minutes

**The Calories:** 145

**The Sodium:** 101mg

**The Potassium:** 461mg

**The Ingredients:**

Sweet potatoes – 4

Extra virgin olive oil – 1 tablespoon

Chili powder – 1.5 teaspoons

Garlic powder - .25 teaspoon

**The Instructions:**

1. Warm the oven to Fahrenheit 425 degrees and prepare a baking sheet by giving it a light coating of non-stick cooking spray.

2. Slice the sweet potatoes into thin slices, no more than one-quarter an inch thick, but as thin as you can possibly get them. This can be done with a sharp knife, but it is easiest to do with a mandolin. Be careful, as it can be easy to accidentally injure yourself.

3. Toss the sliced sweet potatoes in the oil and seasoning until they are evenly coated, and then lay them out on the prepared baking sheet in a single layer. Don't stack the chips, as this will prevent them from crisping up. To do this, you may need to cook the chips in multiple batches or use multiple baking sheets.

4. Roast the chips until both sides are golden and tender, about twenty minutes flipping them once halfway through the cooking time. Once tender, turn the oven's broiler on high and toast them for a minute or two to crisp them up, watching carefully to avoid burning. Serve alone or with your favorite low-sodium condiment for dipping.

# Roasted Sugar Snap Peas

These sugar snap peas are simple, but savory and delicious! Enjoy them fresh from the oven, or store the roasted peas in the fridge and quickly reheat them to serve at a later time.

**The Servings:** 2

**The Time to Prepare/Cook:** 15 minutes

**The Calories:** 110

**The Sodium:** 4mg

**The Potassium:** 238mg

**The Ingredients:**

Sugar snap peas, stems removed - .5 pound

Black pepper, ground - .25 teaspoon

Thyme, dried - .5 teaspoon

Garlic powder - .25 teaspoon

Extra virgin olive oil – 1 tablespoon

**The Instructions:**

1. Warm the oven to Fahrenheit 450 degrees and prepare a baking sheet.

2. Toss together the peas with the oil and seasoning until they are evenly and fully coated. Transfer them to the baking pan.

3. Roast the peas until they are tender and begin to brown around the edges, about eight to twelve minutes. You may want to stir them halfway through cooking. Enjoy while warm.

# Chili Lime Air Fryer Sweet Potatoes

These sweet potatoes are full of flavor reminiscent of traditional Mexican fare. It creates a perfect blend of sweet, savory, smokey, and zesty, which then becomes crispy from cooking in the air fryer. Of course, if you don't have an air fryer you can also use an oven, but the potatoes won't be quite as crispy.

**The Servings:** 4

**The Time to Prepare/Cook:** 20 minutes

**The Calories:** 124

**The Sodium:** 94mg

**The Potassium:** 270mg

**The Ingredients:**

Sweet potatoes – 2

Cumin, ground – 1 teaspoon

Chili powder – 1 tablespoon

Lime juice – 2 teaspoons

Extra virgin olive oil – 2 tablespoons

**The Instructions:**

1. Prepare your oven and potatoes. Warm your air fryer or oven to Fahrenheit 375 degrees. Prepare either the air frying basket or a baking sheet for the oven. Peel your sweet potatoes and then dice them into one-inch cubes.

2. Toss the potatoes together with the remaining ingredients until they are fully and evenly coated. Transfer

the potatoes to either the air frying basket or the baking sheet.

3. Bake the potatoes until crispy, about fifteen to twenty minutes, giving them a good shake or stir every seven minutes. Enjoy warm, or store in the fridge until you plan to eat. Before serving, reheat.

# Garlic Roasted Mushrooms

These mushrooms have a deep umami flavor from the mushrooms roasted with balsamic vinegar, Parmesan cheese, and herbs. You will find them simply irritable! Not only are they a great snack, but you can serve them as an appetizer at parties or as a side dish, as well.

**The Servings:** 3

**The Time to Prepare/Cook:** 35 minutes

**The Calories:** 155

**The Sodium:** 22mg

**The Potassium:** 631mg

**The Ingredients:**

Baby Bella mushrooms – 1 pound

Balsamic vinegar – 2 tablespoons

Extra virgin olive oil – 2 tablespoons

Garlic, minced – 10 cloves

Parmesan cheese, low-sodium, shredded – 2 tablespoons

Black pepper, ground - .5 teaspoon

Oregano, dried – 1 teaspoon

Parsley, fresh, chopped – 2 tablespoons

**The Instructions:**

1. Begin by warming the oven to Fahrenheit 400 degrees and lining a baking sheet with kitchen aluminum.

2. In a bowl, toss the mushrooms with the pepper, orega-

no, balsamic vinegar, and olive oil until fully and evenly coated. Spread the mushrooms onto the prepared baking sheet and place them in the oven.

3. Start by roasting the mushrooms for fifteen minutes. Once this time is up, give the mushrooms a good stir and then sprinkle the Parmesan cheese over the top. Roast the mushrooms for ten more minutes, until the cheese is melted and bubbly and the mushrooms are tender.

4. Remove the mushrooms from the oven, top them with the parsley, and serve warm.

## Greek Lemon Potatoes

These potatoes are fresh, zesty, and comforting. Enjoy the flavor of them alone, or serve them with a fresh Greek Tzatziki sauce. You can easily make these potatoes ahead of time and store them in the fridge. Simply reheat them when ready to serve.

**The Servings:** 8

**The Time to Prepare/Cook:** 55 minutes

**The Calories:** 138

**The Sodium:** 8mg

**The Potassium:** 499mg

**The Ingredients:**

Potatoes, sliced into wedges – 2 pounds

Garlic, minced – 4 cloves

Extra virgin olive oil – 3 tablespoons

Lemon juice - .33 cup

Lemon zest - .5 teaspoon

Water – 1 cup

Oregano, dried – 2 teaspoons

Black pepper, ground - .5 teaspoon

**The Instructions:**

1. Begin by warming your oven to Fahrenheit 400 degrees and preparing a large baking sheet lined with kitchen parchment.

2. Toss the potato wedges with the remaining ingredients until they are evenly and fully coated. Transfer them to the prepared baking sheet.

3. Bake the potatoes until they are tender all the way through and crispy on the outside. This should take forty five minutes. Halfway through the cooking time, give the potatoes a good stir. Serve hot alone or with Tzatziki sauce.

# Broccoli and Cheddar Twice-Baked Potatoes

These potatoes are perfect not only for snacks, but for party appetizers or sports game days. Whenever you choose to enjoy these potatoes, they will feel like a true indulgence—but without the guilt! Just be sure to stick to the recommended serving size, because the sodium in the cheese can add up fast if you go over the recommendation.

**The Servings:** 8

**The Time to Prepare/Cook:** 1 hour and 40 minutes

**The Calories:** 296

**The Sodium:** 260mg

**The Potassium:** 932mg

**The Ingredients:**

Russet potatoes – 4

Greek yogurt, fat-free - .5 cup

Extra virgin olive oil – 3 tablespoons

Black pepper, ground - .5 teaspoon

Garlic powder - .75 teaspoon

Chives, dried - .75 teaspoon

Buttermilk, low-fat – .25 cup

Dill weed, dried - .5 teaspoon

Onion flakes - .5 teaspoon

Onion powder - . 5 teaspoon

Paprika, ground - .5 teaspoon

Broccoli florets, steamed, chopped, divided – 1.5 cups

Cheddar cheese, low-fat – 2 cups

**The Instructions:**

1. Warm the oven to Fahrenheit 400 degrees and line a large baking sheet with kitchen parchment.

2. Place the whole potatoes on the baking sheet and allow them to bake until fork-tender, about one oven. Remove them from the oven, and allow them to cool until they are safe to handle bare handed.

3. Slice the potatoes in half lengthwise. Use a spoon to remove most of the 'meat' of the potato, reserving it in a bowl. When doing this be careful to leave a small amount of potato attached to the peel so that the potato peels stay whole and can be used as a shell for the filling.

4. Use a small amount of the olive oil to coat the potato skins. Place the oiled skins back on the baking sheet and set them aside.

5. Into the bowl with the potato 'meat' add the remaining olive oil, seasonings, buttermilk, Greek and Greek yogurt. Use an electric mixture or potato masher to mash to potatoes until they are mostly smooth and creamy. Stir in the broccoli and three-quarters of the cheese.

6. Take the potato mixture and stuff it back into the prepared shells. Top the potatoes with the remaining cheese and place the baking sheet in the oven. Bake the potatoes until heated through and the cheese is melted, about twenty to twenty-five minutes. Serve

while fresh from the oven or store in the fridge and reheat when ready to enjoy.

## Broccoli Cauliflower Cheese Sticks

These cheese sticks are a low-carb and low-fat, but still delicious! Just give them a try, you are sure to love them. You can easily prepare them ahead of time, and store them in the fridge until ready to enjoy. Just be sure to reheat the cheese sticks before serving.

**The Servings:** 6

**The Time to Prepare/Cook:** 1 hour, 45 minutes

**The Calories:** 80

**The Sodium:** 192mg

**The Potassium:** 447mg

**The Ingredients:**

Cauliflower florets – 5 cups

Broccoli florets – 3 cups

All-purpose flour – 1 tablespoon

Egg – 1

Black pepper, ground - .5 teaspoon

Italian herb seasoning – 1.5 teaspoons

Mozzarella cheese, non-fat, divided – 1 cup

**The Instructions:**

1. Begin by lining a baking sheet with kitchen towels, lining a casserole dish with kitchen parchment, and bringing a large pot of water to a boil.
2. Add the cauliflower and broccoli to the boiling water

for five minutes while being careful to not over cook them. Drain off the water and then transfer the broccoli and cauliflower to the paper towel-lined baking sheet. Allow the vegetables to rest on the baking sheet and dry for an hour, or until fully dried.

3. Preheat your oven to Fahrenheit 400 degrees.

4. Add the dried vegetables into the blender along with the flour, egg, Italian seasoning, and half of the cheese. Pulse the blender until the vegetables are completely blended. Pour the mixture into the casserole dish, smoothing it out until it is even.

5. Place the casserole dish in the oven and cook for twenty minutes before sprinkling the remaining cheese on top. Cook for an additional ten minutes before turning the oven's boiler on high and toasting the cheese for two minutes. Remove from the oven once the cheese is golden, bubbly, and gooey. Slice and serve alone, or with marinara sauce.

## Quinoa Veggie Tots

These tots are a savory and crispy treat, perfect for those who love tater tots. But, these are a healthy alternative that won't worsen your heart-health! Enjoy these alone or by dipping them in your favorite condiments.

**The Servings:** 4

**The Time to Prepare/Cook:** 1 hour

**The Calories:** 328

**The Sodium:** 68mg

**The Potassium:** 640mg

**The Ingredients:**

Quinoa – 1 cup

Carrots, diced – 2

Broccoli florets – 2 cups

Water - .5 cup

Chickpea flour - .75 cup

Garlic powder – 1 teaspoon

Nutritional yeast - .25 cup

Peas - .5 cup

Black pepper, ground - .25 teaspoon

Italian herb seasoning – .5 teaspoon

**The Instructions:**

1. Begin by cooking the quinoa according to the instructions on the packaging. Prepare a baking sheet by

coating it in non-stick cooking spray and warm the oven to Fahrenheit 400 degrees.

2. Meanwhile, whisk together the water and chickpea flour to form a paste. Set it aside while you prepare the other components.

3. In the food processor pulse the peas, carrots, and broccoli until they are chopped into small pieces approximately the same size as the cooked quinoa. Add the chopped vegetables into the bowl with the chickpea flour paste also adding in the garlic powder, nutritional yeast, black pepper, Italian herb seasoning, and cooked quinoa. Combine the mixture well.

4. Take small pieces of the mixture and form each piece into evenly-sized tots, approximately one inch each. They should be similar in size as commercial tater tots. Place the tots one at a time on the prepared baking sheet.

5. Bake the tots until crispy, about forty minutes, flipping them once halfway through the cooking time. They are done when they are golden-brown and crispy. Serve directly from the oven alone or with your favorite condiments.

# Tomato Mozzarella Toast

When you want a special treat, this toast is just what you need! This toast is reminiscent of pizza with its gooey cheese and zesty tomatoes. However, remember not to go over the serving recommendation, as cheese is high in sodium!

**The Servings:** 2

**The Time to Prepare/Cook:** 10 minutes

**The Calories:** 227

**The Sodium:** 391mg

**The Potassium:** 489mg

**The Ingredients:**

Cherry tomatoes – 5 ounces

Tomato paste, low-sodium – 1.5 tablespoons

Tomato sauce, low-sodium – 3 tablespoons

Whole-grain bread – 2 slices

Mozzarella, low-fat, shredded – 2 ounces

Italian herb seasoning - .25 teaspoon

Basil, fresh, chopped - .25 cup

Black pepper, ground - .25 teaspoon

**The Instructions:**

1. Warm the oven to Fahrenheit 400 degrees and place the bread on a baking sheet.
2. In a small bowl, whisk together the tomato paste, tomato sauce, Italian herb seasoning, and black pepper.

Once combined, spread this mixture over the two pieces of bread.

3. Sprinkle the cheese evenly over the bread, followed by the basil, and lastly the cherry tomatoes. Place the bread in the oven and allow it to toast until the cheese is melted, bubbly, and golden-brown, about seven to ten minutes. Serve immediately while warm.

## Parmesan Roasted Carrot Fries

These carrots offer a sweet and savory treat, as the carrots and Parmesan perfectly balance each other out for an irresistible snack. Enjoy these fries alone, or enjoy dipping them in a low-sodium aioli sauce.

**The Servings:** 6

**The Time to Prepare/Cook:** 30 minutes

**The Calories:** 120

**The Sodium:** 110mg

**The Potassium:** 496mg

**The Ingredients:**

Carrots, peeled and sliced into ¼" fries – 2 pounds

Extra virgin olive oil – 1 tablespoon

Parmesan, low-sodium, shredded - .5 cup

Black pepper, ground - .5 teaspoon

**The Instructions:**

1. Warm the oven to Fahrenheit 425 degrees and line a baking sheet with kitchen parchment.
2. Toss together the carrot fries with all of the ingredients and transfer them to the baking sheet, spreading them out into a single layer.
3. Place the carrots in the oven and roast them until they are golden-brown, about twenty minutes. Halfway through the cooking time mix the carrots around so that they cook evenly. Remove from the oven and serve warm.

## Frozen Banana Yoghurt Bites

Keep these yogurt bites prepared in the freezer and you will always have a sweet and satisfying snack ready and on hand! To take one on the road, simply place a couple cups in a plastic bag, placing the bag inside a small chilled cooler.

**The Servings:** 4

**The Time to Prepare/Cook:** 7 minutes

**The Calories:** 76

**The Sodium:** 103mg

**The Potassium:** 791mg

**The Ingredients:**

Banana, ripe – 1

Greek yogurt, vanilla, fat-free – 1 cup

**The Instructions:**

1. Place silicone muffin liners inside a muffin pan and divide the Greek yogurt between them. You want to fill each cup halfway, so you should be left with four cups.

2. Slice the peeled banana into slices, and place the slices inside of the four muffin cups. Use a spoon to push the banana slices down, so that they are partially submerged.

3. Place the muffin cups in the freezer and allow them to freeze for a few hours, until hardened. Once hard, remove the yogurt cups from the silicone and place them in a container to store in the freezer until you are ready to enjoy them.

# Peanut Butter Energy Bites

Keep these energy bites stored in the freezer or a cold bag to take on the go, and you will always have a sweet burst of energy nearby to help you throughout your day. If you love chocolate and peanut butter cups, then you are sure to love these energy bites, as well!

**The Servings:** 12

**The Time to Prepare/Cook:** 20 minutes

**The Calories:** 210

**The Sodium:** 36mg

**The Potassium:** 149mg

**The Ingredients:**

Peanut butter, creamy, low-sodium - .66 cup

Rolled oats – 1 cup

Semi-sweet chocolate chips - .5 cup

Flaxseeds, ground - .5 cup

Honey – 2 tablespoons

**The Instructions:**

1. Combine the peanut butter and other ingredients together in a bowl. Once combined, place the bowl in the refrigerator and allow it to chill for at least fifteen minutes, until the mixture is somewhat firm and easier to handle.

2. Use a spoon to scoop the mixture into twelve evenly-sized pieces. Roll them between your hands to form

balls. Place the energy bites in a container and store them in the fridge until ready to serve.

## Cinnamon Apple Chips

These apple chips may take a bit of time to prepare, but most of their work is not hands-on time, which means they can be cooking while you go about your day. Preparing these chips ahead of time is well worth the effort, as they are a delicious snack that you can easily enjoy at home or on the go!

**The Servings:** 4

**The Time to Prepare/Cook:** 2 hours and 45 minutes

**The Calories:** 102

**The Sodium:** 2mg

**The Potassium:** 202mg

**The Ingredients:**

Cinnamon, ground – 2 teaspoons

Red apples, peeled and sliced 1/8" thick – 4

Brown sugar – 1 teaspoon

**The Instructions:**

1. Warm the oven to Fahrenheit 200 degrees and coat a couple large baking sheets with non-stick cooking spray.

2. Toss the thinly sliced apples with the brown sugar and cinnamon until they are evenly coated, and then spread them over the baking sheets in a single layer. Don't overcrowd the pan, otherwise the apples will be unable to cook evenly or get crispy.

3. Bake the chips until they are soft yet still crisp, about two to three hours. Once done cooking, allow the ap-

ples to cool completely at room temperature before storing them, to avoid humidity buildup in the container. You can store these chips up to four days in an airtight container.

# CHAPTER 7

# SAUCES, GRAVIES, AND SEASONINGS

Most prepared sauces, gravies, and seasonings on the market are full of sodium, making them impossible for people with high blood pressure to use. But, there is no need to worry! Many of these ingredients are much more simple to create than you might think. You can make them whenever you might need them, but you can also make them ahead of time and store them in the freezer or pantry.

## Taco Seasoning

While this taco seasoning may say it makes eight 'servings,' it actually makes much more than this, really giving you your money's worth! What this recipe makes eight of is the taco seasoning packets. This means that if you were to purchase eight taco seasoning packets at the store it would be equal to the amount of taco seasoning in this recipe. However, this recipe does not contain any salt, making it heart-healthy!

When using this seasoning to make taco meat or even taco tofu, use seven teaspoons for every pound of meat or meat replacement.

**The Servings:** 8

**The Time to Prepare/Cook:** 2 minutes

**The Calories:** 153

**The Sodium:** 710mg

**The Potassium:** 791mg

**The Ingredients:**

Cumin, ground - .75 cup

Chili powder – 1.5 cups

Garlic powder – 2 tablespoons

Onion powder – 2 tablespoons

Paprika – 6 tablespoons

Cornstarch – 6 tablespoons

**The Instructions:**

1. Stir together all of the ingredients in a bowl until fully combined, and then transfer the mixture to an airtight container for storage.

2. To use the seasoning, brown a pound of lean turkey and then add in seven teaspoons of taco seasoning and three-quarters of a cup of water. Allow the meat, seasoning, and water to simmer together until the water has evaporated and created a sauce coating the meat.

## Marinara Sauce

Whether you are hoping to make pasta, spaghetti squash, rice, or anything else, marinara sauce is the perfect topping! Enjoy this marinara sauce straight, or add some ground turkey or meatballs for an extra special sauce.

**The Servings:** 6

**The Time to Prepare/Cook:** 55 minutes

**The Calories:** 138

**The Sodium:** 38mg

**The Potassium:** 610mg

**The Ingredients:**

Crushed tomatoes, low-sodium – 28 ounces

Water – 1 cup

Basil leaves, chopped – 5

Onion, diced - .33 cup

Garlic, minced – 6 cloves

Oregano, dried - .5 teaspoon

Red pepper flakes - .25 teaspoon

Extra virgin olive oil - .25 cup

**The Instructions:**

1. Over medium heat in a large pot heat together the onions until they are translucent, about five minutes. Add in the red pepper flakes and garlic and cook and additional minute, until fragrant. Be careful not to

burn the garlic or red pepper!

2. Pour the crushed tomatoes tomatoes and water into the pot, giving it a good stir. Allow the sauce to simmer and thicken on medium-low until most of the water has evaporated, about thirty minutes.

3. Stir the herbs into the pot and simmer the sauce for fifteen more minutes before removing the marinara from the heat. Serve the marinara immediately or freeze it until ready to use.

## Easy Homemade Salsa

This salsa is incredibly simple, quick, and delicious! You can even easily customize the spiciness level. If you want, you can leave the jalapeno out of the salsa. Or, for mild, you can remove the jalapeno seeds (where most of the spiciness is contained) and only add the fruit of the pepper to the salsa. If you want spicy, add both the pepper and the seeds to your salsa. And, if you want ultra-spicy salsa, then you can even add in a Serrano or even a Habanero pepper. The same is true if you want a sweet and spicy salsa, along with adding in your choice of peppers, you could also add in peach, mango, or pineapple. The choices are yours and the options are endless!

**The Servings:** 4

**The Time to Prepare/Cook:** 5 minutes

**The Calories:** 26

**The Sodium:** 8mg

**The Potassium:** 319mg

**The Ingredients:**

Roma tomatoes, diced – 8

Green onions, finely diced – 2

Jalapeno, diced – 1

Cilantro, fresh, chopped – 2 tablespoons

Lime juice – 1 tablespoon

**The Instructions:**

1. Toss all of the ingredients together in a bowl and give the salsa a taste. Adjust the salsa as you would like,

adding more ingredients if you want.

2. Serve the salsa immediately or store it in the fridge for up to twenty-four hours before enjoying.

# Barbecue Sauce

Most barbecue sauce you can purchase is full of an obscene amount of sodium, but it doesn't have to be. In as little as thirty-five minutes, you can make a simple and delicious homemade barbecue sauce. Don't have time to make your own every time you need to use it? No worries! You can easily make this sauce and store it in an airtight jar in the fridge for up to a month or in the freezer for up to six months.

**The Servings:** 12

**The Time to Prepare/Cook:** 35 minutes

**The Calories:** 60

**The Sodium:** 60mg

**The Potassium:** 367mg

**The Ingredients:**

Ketchup, low-sodium - .5 cup

Tomato paste, low-sodium – 12 ounces

Water – 2 cups

Lemon juice – 2 tablespoons

Apple cider vinegar – 2 tablespoons

Brown sugar - .25 cup

Chili powder – 2 tablespoons

Onion powder – 1 tablespoon

Paprika – 1 teaspoon

Black pepper, ground - .5 teaspoon

Mustard seed, ground – 1 teaspoon

Garlic powder – .5 teaspoon

**The Instructions:**

1. Whisk together all of the barbecue sauce ingredients in a large saucepan on the stove and bring it to a boil over medium heat.

2. Cover the pot with a lid, reduce the heat to low, and allow the sauce to simmer for thirty minutes. Remove the sauce from the heat and allow it to cool before storing.

# Easy 5-Minute Gravy

This gravy is incredibly easy to make and delicious! While this gravy is vegan, you can also make it with any low-sodium broth to make different flavors, such as turkey or chicken. Do you need to make gluten-free broth? Simple, all you have to do is use brown rice flour instead of wheat flour!

**The Servings:** 8

**The Time to Prepare/Cook:** 5 minutes

**The Calories:** 32

**The Sodium:** 103mg

**The Potassium:** 13mg

**The Ingredients:**

Vegetable broth, low-sodium – 2 cups

Soy sauce, low-sodium – 1 tablespoon

Onion powder - .75 teaspoon

Mustard seed, ground - .25 teaspoon

Nutritional yeast – 3 tablespoons

All-purpose flour - .25 cup

**The Instructions:**

1. Whisk together all of the ingredients in a saucepan until the flour is dissolved without any flour clumps. Bring the liquid to a boil over medium-high heat.
2. Continue to stir the gravy as it thickens to your desired consistency, and then remove it from the heat and serve warm. Use immediately or store in the fridge for up to one week.

# Herbs de Provence Herb Seasoning

This is a delicious and warm French herbal seasoning that is unlike any other. It may seem odd to add lavender flowers to the blend, but the small amount won't stick out too strongly in your food, it perfectly accentuates the other herbs. Please give it a try, it will become your new favorite go-to seasoning for meats, fish, salads, sauces, and most anything else.

**The Servings:** 43

**The Time to Prepare/Cook:** 2 minutes

**The Calories:** 2

**The Sodium:** 1mg

**The Potassium:** 15mg

**The Ingredients:**

Basil, dried – 2 tablespoons

Thyme, dried – 2 tablespoons

Parsley, dried – 2 tablespoons

Oregano, dried – 1 tablespoon

Tarragon, dried – 1 tablespoon

Rosemary, dried – 2 tablespoons

Fennel seed – 1 tablespoon

Marjoram, dried – 2 tablespoons

Lavender buds, dried – 2 tablespoons

Bay leaf, dried, ground – 1 teaspoon

**The Instructions:**

1. Ensure all of your herbs are ground to the same consistency. This is especially important for the rosemary, fennel seed, and rosemary. To do this, run your herbs through a spice grinder or even a coffee grinder.

2. Stir all of the herbs together until combined and then store in a airtight glass jar. Place the jar in a cool and dark location where sunlight and heat won't damage it, and it should last a year.

## Teriyaki Sauce

While this teriyaki sauce is much lower in sodium than commercial varieties, keep in mind that even 'low-sodium' soy sauce still contains quite a bit of sodium! In fact, the most popular brand, Kikkoman's Less Sodium Soy Sauce 590mg of sodium for every tablespoon. So, enjoy this teriyaki sauce in moderation and only when you are well under your day's sodium limit.

**The Servings:** 8

**The Time to Prepare/Cook:** 5 minutes

**The Calories:** 40

**The Sodium:** 380mg

**The Potassium:** 61mg

**The Ingredients:**

Pineapple juice - .33 cup

Soy sauce, low-sodium - .33 cup

Honey – 3 tablespoons

Water – 3 tablespoons

Rice wine vinegar – 2 tablespoons

Garlic, minced – 1 clove

Cornstarch – 2 teaspoons

Black pepper, ground - .25 teaspoon

Ginger root, minced – 1 teaspoon

**The Instructions:**

1. Pour all of the ingredients together into a saucepan and whisk them together so that no clumps remain.
2. Bring the sauce to a boil over medium-high heat, and then reduce the heat to medium and allow the sauce to thicken and simmer for five minutes. Once the sauce has thickened remove it from the heat. Use it immediately, or store it in the fridge for up to a month before using.

# CHAPTER 8
# BEVERAGES

In this chapter, you are provided with refreshing drinks and smoothies that will be the perfect reward after a long day. You don't have to struggle with cravings for drinks full of sugar and saturated fats when you can always make these sweet treats.

## Lavender Lemonade

While you could certainly make regular lemonade with this recipe by simply omitting the lavender flowers, if you have the chance I urge you to try to make the lavender lemonade as intended. The subtle floral flavor of the lavender perfectly pairs with the lemon, making it irresistible.

**The Servings:** 8

**The Time to Prepare/Cook:** 5 minutes

**The Calories:** 13

**The Sodium:** 1mg

**The Potassium:** 63mg

**The Ingredients:**

Truvia sugar-free sweetener – 1 cup

Boiling water – 1.5 cups

Cold water – 6 cups

Lemon juice, fresh – 2 cups

Lavender sprigs – 6

Ice cubes

**The Instructions:**

1. In a pitcher stir together the boiling water with the lavender and Truvia sweetener until the sweetener has dissolved. Allow the mixture to cool and steep for an hour.

2. Remove and discard the lavender sprigs, straining the mixture, if needed. Into the pitcher stir the lemon, cold water, and some ice until combined.

3. Serve the lemonade alone or with a garnish of lavender.

## Pink Drink Strawberry Refresher

This recipe uses coconut milk from the carton. This is an important distinction to keep in mind, as canned coconut milk is higher in fat, which not only means more calories but also more saturated fats in your diet.

**The Servings:** 1

**The Time to Prepare/Cook:** 2 minutes

**The Calories:** 40

**The Sodium:** 22mg

**The Potassium:** 155mg

**The Ingredients:**

Strawberry sparkling water, unsweetened – 1 cup

Coconut milk, unsweetened, from the carton - .5 cup

Freeze-dried strawberries - .25 cup

**The Instructions:**

1. Crush the freeze-dried strawberries and add them into a glass. Pour the strawberry sparkling water over the top and wait for the carbonation bubbles to go down.

2. Pour the coconut milk over the top and give the glass a good stir. Serve alone or add in some ice cubes.

# Chocolate Banana Smoothie

This smoothie is great for when you are tight on time and need a smoothie rather than a meal, because it has more than enough nutrients and calories to replace a meal! Yet, unlike many meal replacement shakes, this smoothie is full of real whole foods and delicious flavor.

**The Servings:** 2

**The Time to Prepare/Cook:** 3 minutes

**The Calories:** 533

**The Sodium:** 117mg

**The Potassium:** 1135mg

**The Ingredients:**

Almond milk, unsweetened – 1 cup

Cocoa powder – 2 tablespoons

Rolled oats - .5 cup

Bananas, frozen – 2

Chia seeds – 2 tablespoons

Almond butter, low-sodium – 3 tablespoons

Greek yogurt, non-fat - .5 cup

Almond extract - .125 teaspoon

Vanilla extract - .25 teaspoon

**The Instructions:**

1. Add the rolled oats and chia seeds to the blender, and then pulse them until they have formed a fine flour.

2. Add the remaining ingredients into the blender and blend until it is completely smooth without any chunks, scraping the sides of the blender with a spatula as needed. Serve immediately while cold.

# Coffee Banana Smoothie

This smoothie will give you a wonderful caffeine boost, unless you choose to use decaffeinated coffee. Whether you choose to make this smoothie caffeinated or caffeine-free, you will love the flavor and sweet treat of this smoothie! You will never need to pay eight dollars for a cup of coffee again.

**The Servings:** 1

**The Time to Prepare/Cook:** 3 minutes

**The Calories:** 222

**The Sodium:** 114mg

**The Potassium:** 1040mg

**The Ingredients:**

Skim milk – 1 cup

Banana – 1

Cocoa powder – 1 tablespoon

Brewed coffee, frozen into cubes – 1 cup

**The Instructions:**

1. To make your frozen coffee cubes, all you have to do is pour a cup of coffee into ice cube trays, allowing them to freeze for at least two hours until solid.

2. Into the blender add the coffee ice cubes and remaining ingredients, blending until completely smooth without any banana clumps. Serve immediately while still cold.

# Cherry Limeade Detox Drink

This cherry limeade drink uses apple cider vinegar, which has many amazing health benefits, including the ability to detox the body! But, don't worry, the vinegar is not strong, as you only have a small amount in the drink which is then combined with cherries, lime juice, and sweetener. You will love this cherry limeade.

**The Servings:** 2 minutes

**The Time to Prepare/Cook:** 2 minutes

**The Calories:** 29

**The Sodium:** 8mg

**The Potassium:** 105mg

**The Ingredients:**

Lime juice – 1 tablespoon

Apple cider vinegar – 2 tablespoons

Water – 3 cups

Sweet cherries, frozen - .5 cup

Stevia sweetener drops – 6 drops

**The Instructions:**

1. Pour all of the ingredients into a blender and blend until completely smooth. Serve over ice while cold and enjoy.

# CHAPTER 9

# DESSERTS

Every good and healthy diet requires balance, and thankfully the DASH diet is well balanced, as long as an individual follows the diet's recommendations. This means that you can even indulge in the occasional sweets, though they should only be a treat you indulge in from time to time. You can feel good knowing that the desserts in this chapter are healthier than the alternative, meaning you can enjoy them more frequently without impacting your health as much as the alternative would.

## Oatmeal Chocolate Chip Cookies

Who doesn't love a chewy oatmeal and chocolate chip cookie? I sure do! But, if chocolate isn't your thing, you can replace it with raisins, walnuts, or even coconut! Feel free to add your favorite mix-ins, just keep in mind that will change the nutritional information.

**The Servings:** 24

**The Time to Prepare/Cook:** 25 minutes

**The Calories:** 151

**The Sodium:** 5mg

**The Potassium:** 134mg

**The Ingredients:**

Egg, room temperature – 1

Butter, light, softened – .25 cup

Coconut oil, softened - .25 cup

Truvia Brown Sugar Blend – 1 cup

Vanilla extract – 2 teaspoons

.75 cup

sodium – 1 teaspoon

olate chips - .75 cup

**The Instructions:**

2. Warm the oven to Fahrenheit 350 degrees and line two large baking sheets with kitchen parchment or silicone kitchen mats.

3. In one bowl, combine the whole-wheat flour, oats, and baking soda, and then set it aside.

4. In another large bowl, use a hand beater to mix together and cream the coconut oil and butter. Once fluffy, add in the Truvia and continue beating until the Truvia crystals have dissolved into the butter mixture and become extra fluffy, about two minutes. Beat in the vanilla extract and the egg.

5. Add the flour mixture to the butter mixture folding it until combined. Once it has formed a cohesive dough, fold in the chocolate chips.

6. Use a cookie scoop or a spoon to level out evenly-sized dough balls, each equal to about two tablespoons of dough. Roll each piece of dough into a ball between your hands and then place them on the baking sheet, each two inches apart.

7. Place the baking sheet in the oven and bake the cookies until the edges are set but the middle is still soft, about eight to ten minutes. Remove the pans from the oven and allow the cookies to cool on them for one

minute, before gently removing them and transferring them to a wire cooling rack.

8. Enjoy the cookies warm or store them in an airtight container for up to a week.

# Fig Bars

If you have ever liked the store-bought fig cookies, then you will absolutely love these fig bars! They are easy to make, as the filling is made with fig jam, which you can purchase pre-made. If you choose to prepare these bars, then you are in for a real treat!

**The Servings:** 9

**The Time to Prepare/Cook:** 50 minutes

**The Calories:** 277

**The Sodium:** 5mg

**The Potassium:** 148mg

**The Ingredients:**

Butter, light, room-temperature - .5 cup

Rolled oats – 1 cup

Baking soda, low-sodium - .25 teaspoon

Whole-wheat flour - .75 cup

Truvia Brown Sugar Blend - .5 cup

Fig jam – 10 ounces

**The Instructions:**

1. Warm the oven to Fahrenheit 350 degrees and prepare an eight-inch square baking dish with kitchen parchment and non-stick cooking spray.

2. In a medium bowl, combine the rolled oats, baking soda, and whole-wheat flour. Once combined, cut in the butter with a pastry cutter until it forms a crumbly mixture with butter in pea-sized pieces throughout the mixture.

3. Take two cups of the crumble mixture and press it into the bottom of the prepared pan as a crust. Spread the fig jam over center of the crust, stopping just short of the edges of the crust. You should be left with a one-quarter inch of clean crust around the edges, and the jam in the center of the crust.

4. Sprinkle the remaining crumble over the top of the pan, lightly pressing it into the jam so that it sticks.

5. Bake the bars in the warm oven until the crumble is lightly browned, about thirty-five to forty minutes. Allow the bars to cool completely before slicing into them and cutting them into nine evenly-sized bars.

## Whole-Grain Molasses Cookies

Who doesn't love a warm molasses cookie? Whether you are enjoying these during the holidays, when you're feeling ill to help settle your stomach, or just to enjoy a delicious treat anytime of the year, you are sure to love these cookies!

**The Servings:** 24

**The Time to Prepare/Cook:** 25 minutes

**The Calories:** 121

**The Sodium:** 5mg

**The Potassium:** 135mg

**The Ingredients:**

Egg – 1

Molasses - .25 cup

Truvia Brown Sugar Sweetener – 1 cup

Extra virgin olive oil - .66 cup

Whole-wheat flour – 2 cups

Baking soda, low-sodium – 2 teaspoons

Nutmeg, ground - .25 teaspoon

Cloves, ground - .5 teaspoon

Ginger, ground – 1 teaspoon

Cinnamon, ground – 1.5 teaspoons

**The Instructions:**

1. Warm the oven to Fahrenheit 350 degrees and prepare

a couple large baking sheets by lining them with kitchen parchment.

2. In a large bowl, beat together the egg, molasses, Truvia, and olive oil until combined.

3. In a medium bowl, combine the whole-wheat flour, baking soda, and spices until evenly combined. Fold this mixture into the wet mixture until it forms a cohesive dough.

4. Use a cookie scoop to create one-inch dough balls. You can now either place these dough balls on the prepared pan two inches apart, or you can first roll each one into a little Truvia Sugar Free sweetener for a little extra sweetness and texture.

5. Bake the cookies until they are set around the edges but soft in the middle, about eight to ten minutes. Allow the cookies to cool on the pan for one minute before transferring to a wire cooling rack.

# Chocolate Peanut Butter Oatmeal No-Bake Cookies

These no-bake cookies are incredibly and don't even need an oven! Children and adults alike are sure to love this traditional sweet treat made with a healthy twist.

**The Servings:** 15

**The Time to Prepare/Cook:** 40 minutes

**The Calories:** 226

**The Sodium:** 3mg

**The Potassium:** 196mg

**The Ingredients:**

Maple syrup - .5 cup

Coconut oil - .5 cup

Peanut butter, low-sodium - .5 cup

Cocoa powder - .25 cup

Vanilla extract - .5 teaspoon

Rolled oats – 2 cups

**The Instructions:**

1. Prepare a baking sheet by lining it with kitchen parchment or a silicone kitchen mat, and then set it aside.

2. Stir together all of the ingredients in a bowl until they are well combined.

3. Use a cookie scoop or a spoon to create evenly-sized

dough balls, approximately one-inch in size. Transfer the balls to the prepared baking sheet and then place it in the freezer until they are set, about thirty to sixty minutes.

4. Store the cookies in an airtight container in the fridge or freezer until you plan to eat them.

# Carrot Cake Banana Bread

This carrot cake has a twist, which is a sweet and delicious banana mixed in, along with walnuts. However, you can also add in some other carrot cake favorites, if you want, such as coconut and raisins. However you make this dessert, you are sure to love it!

**The Servings:** 12

**The Time to Prepare/Cook:** 50 minutes

**The Calories:** 190

**The Sodium:** 9mg

**The Potassium:** 310mg

**The Ingredients:**

Skim milk - .25 cup

Extra virgin olive oil - .25 cup

Vanilla extract – 2 teaspoons

Maple syrup - .5 cup

Whole-wheat flour – 2 cups

Cinnamon – 1 teaspoon

Baking soda, low-sodium – 1 teaspoon

Baking powder, low-sodium - .75 teaspoon

Nutmeg, ground - .125 teaspoon

Banana, mashed – 1.5 cups

Carrot, shredded - .5 cup

Walnuts, chopped - .25 cup

**The Instructions:**

1. Prepare the oven to Fahrenheit 350 degrees and line a nine-by-five inch loaf pan with kitchen parchment.

2. In a large bow, combine the whole wheat flour, baking powder, baking soda, spices, and walnuts.

3. In another bowl, whisk together the remaining wet ingredients. Once combined, add in the flour mixture and fold the batter together until it is evenly combined.

4. Pour the batter into the prepared baking pan and place it in the oven to cook, about forty minutes. The dessert is ready when you insert a toothpick in the center of the bread and it comes out clean.

5. Remove the bread from the oven and allow it to cool for five minutes before removing it from the pan and transfer it to a wire cooling rack. Allow the bread to fully cool before slicing. Serve immediately, or store

in an airtight container at room temperature for up to three days.

# Baked Pears with Walnuts

These pears are tender and sweet, perfectly complimenting the warm and nutty walnuts and cinnamon. You will absolutely love this sweet treat. Enjoy it alone or with a small amount of vanilla yogurt for a creamy touch.

**The Servings:** 2

**The Time to Prepare/Cook:** 35 minutes

**The Calories:** 218

**The Sodium:** 3mg

**The Potassium:** 291mg

**The Ingredients:**

Pears, halved – 2

Maple syrup – 2 teaspoons

Walnuts, chopped - .25 cup

Cinnamon – 1 teaspoon

**The Instructions:**

1. Warm the oven to Fahrenheit 375 degrees and prepare a baking sheet or casserole dish for the pears.

2. Slice the pears in half and use a spoon to remove the core. On the backside with the peel, cut a small sliver off of the pear so that it can sit on its back evenly without falling over.

3. Arrange the pears on the baking sheet and then sprinkle and walnuts over the top and then drizzle the maple syrup over it all.

4. Bake the pears until softened and lightly browned, about twenty-five minutes. Remove the pan from the oven and serve warm. If you want to, you can store the pears in the fridge for up to five days and then reheat them before serving.

# CONCLUSION

The DASH diet has long been used to treat high blood pressure and improve weight loss. But that is not all! This diet not only has a long use in improving health, but it has also been extensively studied, proving that it is a safe and reliable method, so much so that doctors routinely recommend it for their patients with high blood pressure. This means you can trust in the DASH diet and its benefits, knowing that it will provide you with the results you need to see.

It can be difficult to begin a new diet or lifestyle, but you can take it one step at a time. Don't rush yourself if you don't have to. Instead, you can make one small change at a time until you fully adopt a full DASH diet and an accompanying healthy lifestyle.

What are you waiting for? You have all the tools you need to succeed! Armed with the information in this book, over seventy-five delicious recipes, and a 30-day meal plan, you can be well on your way to success in no time. All you have to do is begin.

Lastly, please remember to always discuss your diet and lifestyle with your doctor. The information in this book is not meant to diagnose, prescribe, or treat.

Made in the USA
Middletown, DE
18 September 2020